Kitchen Wizard

For all of us who could use
are some wizard tricks to tı
irresistible delights to pleas
satisfy the rumbling tummy
Jarvis shows us how to wie
complete meal to suit every occasion and every whim. So should you suddenly feel like a brunch with Dorothy in the Land of Oz, a picnic beside the Mississippi with Huck Finn, tea in Lilliput with Gulliver or even a snack with a band of roguish smugglers, put on your magic cooking cap, pick up your whizz stick and away you go . . .

SOME MORE TITLES IN LIONS

Born Free *Joy Adamson*
Living Free *Joy Adamson*
Forever Free *Joy Adamson*
Mr Popper's Penguins *Richard and Florence Atwater*
Jenny and the Cat Club *Esther Averill*
A Bear Called Paddington *Michael Bond*
and ten other titles
Susannah of the Mounties *Muriel Denison*
The Donkey Rustlers *Gerald Durrell*
The Talking Parcel *Gerald Durrell*
My Father's Dragon *Ruth Gannett*
Sea Star *Marguerite Henry*
King of the Wind *Marguerite Henry*
The Phantom Tollbooth *Norton Juster*
The Tree that Sat Down *Beverley Nichols*
The Stream that Stood Still *Beverley Nichols*
The Mountain of Magic *Beverley Nichols*
Mind Your Own Business *Michael Rosen*
Ballet Shoes for Anna *Noel Streatfield*
Mary Poppins *P. L. Travers*
Down with Skool! *Geoffrey Willans and Ronald Searle*
The Boy Who Sprouted Antlers *John Yeoman*

KITCHEN WIZARD

by DEBORAH JARVIS

illustrated by Arthur Robins

FONTANA: LIONS ORIGINAL

To Wizard's Editor –
who never once complained
of indigestion

First published in Lions 1977
by William Collins Sons and Co. Ltd
14 St James's Place, London SW1

Printed in Great Britain
by William Collins Sons and Co. Ltd, Glasgow

Inside

Note to all Kitchen Wizards

Before you dabble in the delights of Kitchen Wizardry, cast a glance at these few tips first .

Don't go rushing off the minute you see a recipe and use magic to turn mountains into dough hills. This is cheating and will only lead to lumpy biscuits. It will also start you off on the wrong foot with the High Council of Kitchen Wizards who are sticklers for the Rules. They complain that young Wizards nowadays don't know the first thing about kitchen-magic and can't tell a wand from a whizz-stick*. They insist that the art of cooking is found first in your *head*, and then in the recipe mumbo-jumbo.

The secret, then, is to get a headstart. Find your Wizard cap and put it on straight. Then let your mind float along the lines of what and where you would like to eat.

* wooden spoon

If you've been overdoing the spells and potions lately, why not join Huckleberry Finn for a picnic beside the Mississippi? Without taking a step, lie back and conjure up the smell of bacon cooking over hickory logs, the hooting of steam boats on the river and Huck's cursing as he stubs his toe on a tree-stump. Then put yourself in the picture by rustling up a batch of Barefoot Bread or a few pieces of Hickory Chicken.

To master this Kitchen Wizardry, be prepared for all challenges. You could be called upon at any moment to produce a pudding out of thin air or a rabbit stew from your cap. Never go near a kitchen without brushing up on your Basic Abracadabra and tucking a few Tricks of the Trade up your sleeve. Once you have done this, your kitchen-magic will be foolproof.

Basic Abracadabra

BAKE
Cook in the oven.

BASTE
Pour or brush liquid from time to time over food as it cooks.

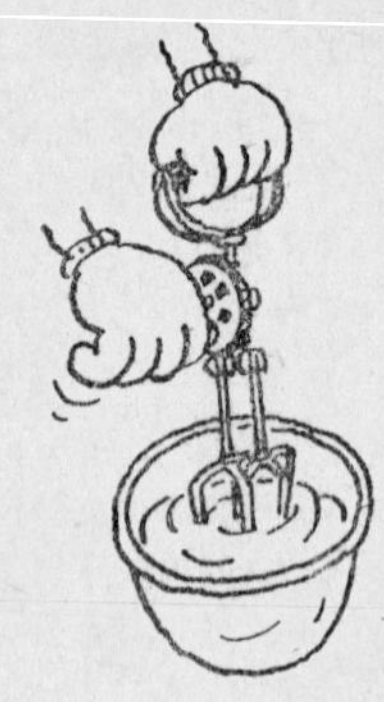

BEAT
Mix vigorously in a circular motion to make a mixture smooth – either with a rotary or electric beater or a whizz-stick (wooden spoon).

BLEND
Mix two or more ingredients together until it is impossible to tell one from the other.

BOIL
Heat a liquid until it bubbles furiously and lets off steam.

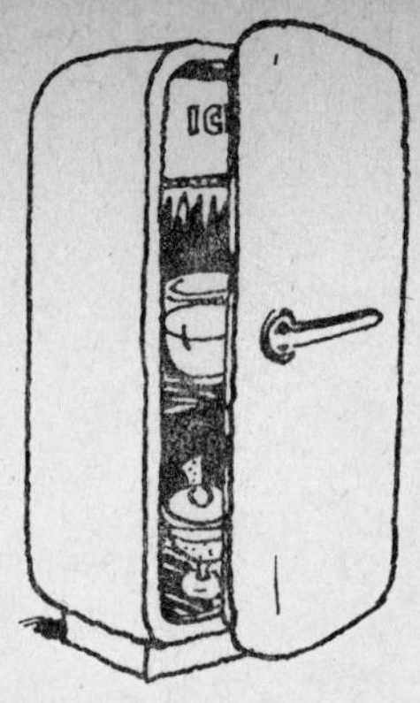

CHILL
Put in a refrigerator or a cold place to cool.

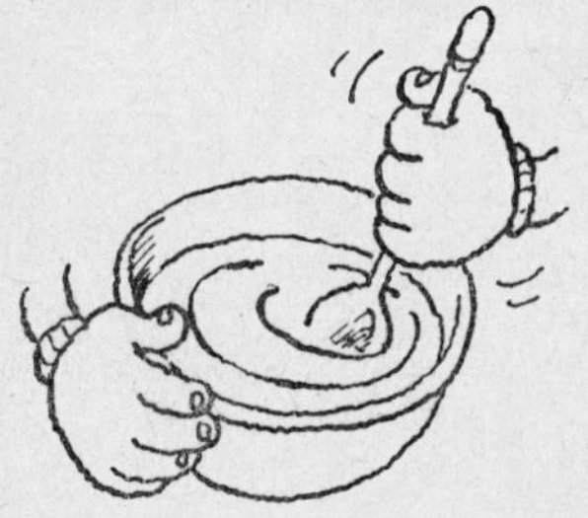

CREAM
Beat sugar and soft butter (or margarine) until light, soft and fluffy with a whizz-stick (wooden spoon). Sit down to do this and hold the mixing bowl in your lap

DICE
Cut into small squares.

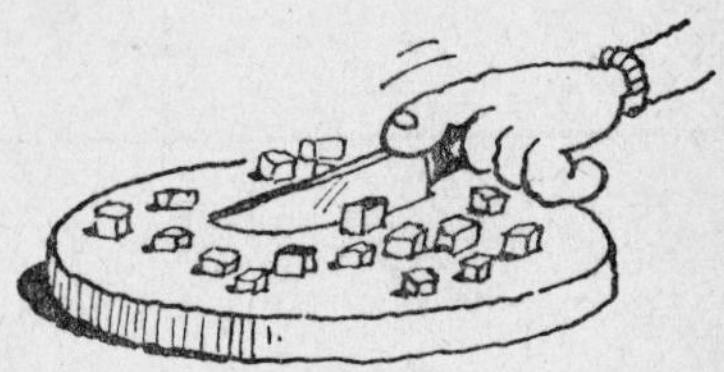

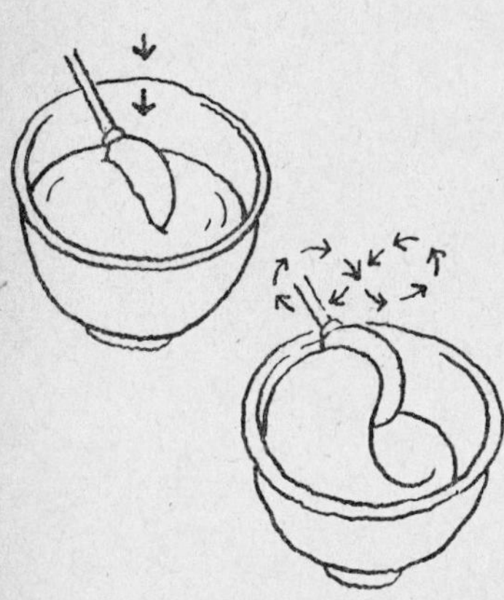

FOLD
Mix a light ingredient into a heavier one very gently with a knife or metal spoon. Cut into mixture with edge of spoon, down across the bottom of bowl and up over the surface.

FRY
Cook in hot fat in a frying-pan on top of the stove.

GRATE
Cut into small pieces by rubbing against a grater

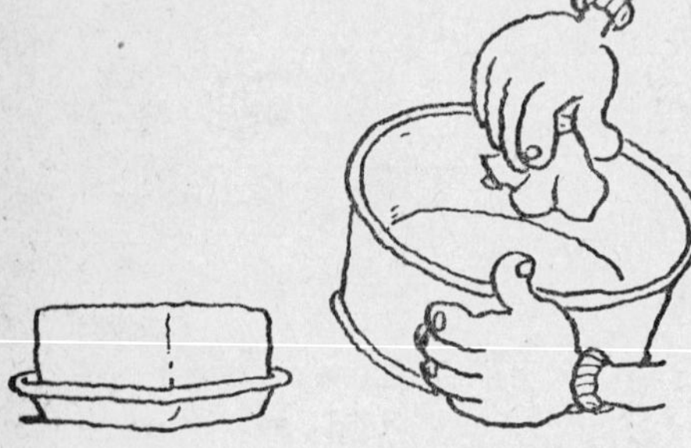

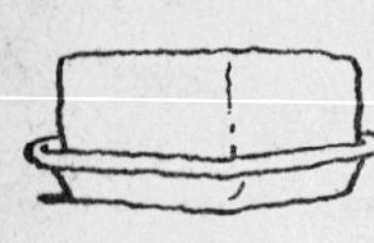

GREASE
To oil or butter the bottom and sides of a baking tin to prevent sticking.

KNEAD
Handle dough by folding, turning and then pressing it down with heel of hand.

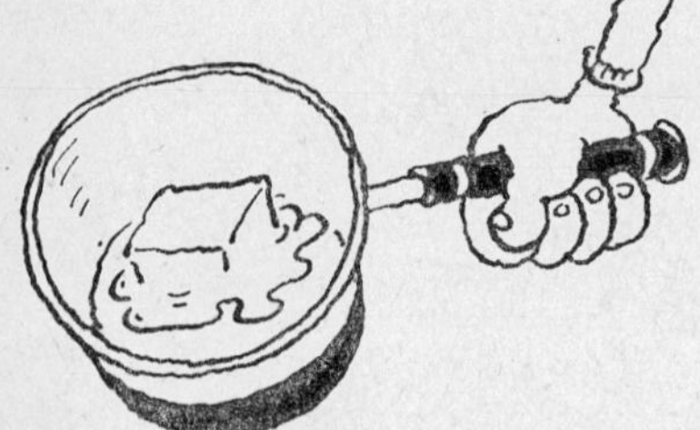

MELT
Turn a solid ingredient into a liquid one by heating it (either in a saucepan on top of the stove or in a pan in the oven)

PRE-HEAT
Turn the oven on before you start mixing so that it will be the right temperature when you are ready to bake

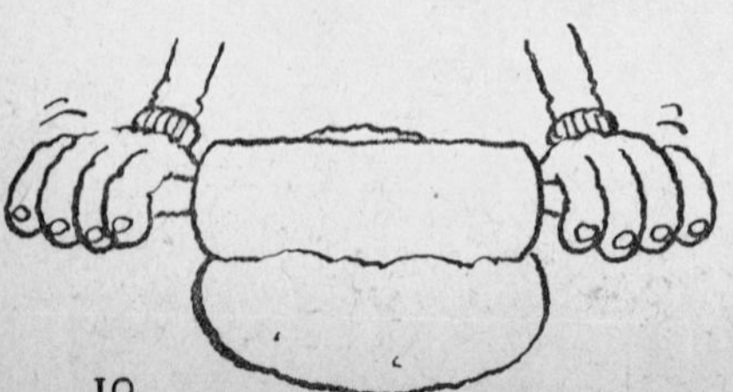

ROLL OUT
Roll dough out on to lightly floured counter with rolling pin (dusted with flour) until the dough is completely flat and the right thickness

RUB IN

Cut off small pieces of butter and drop into flour mixture. Rub fat and flour together between your fingertips, lifting out of bowl slightly to get as much air in as possible. Do this until mixture looks like fine breadcrumbs.

SIFT

Put flour or other dry ingredients through a sieve to get rid of lumps.

SIMMER

Cook liquid in a saucepan over low heat so that it bubbles very slowly.

TEST

If a toothpick stuck into the centre of a loaf or cake comes out clean, then it is ready to take out of the oven.

WHIP

Beat with a whisk, rotary or electric beater until light, fluffy and full of air.

Tricks of the Trade

Always coax, wheedle or cajole a Senior Chef to stand by while you are cooking – just in case you need an extra hand or help tasting.

Beware of recipes with lots of ingredients. Make sure you have them all *before* you start or you may never get finished!

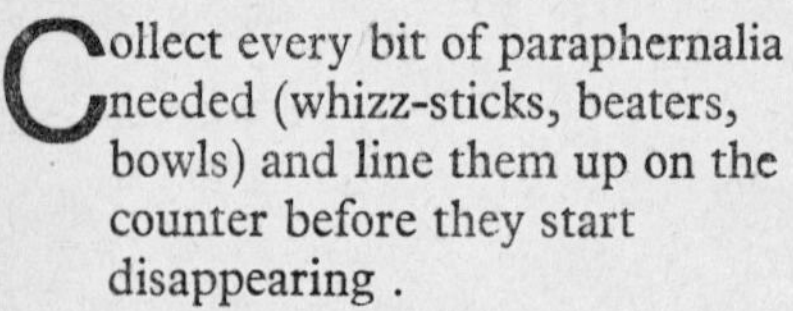

Collect every bit of paraphernalia needed (whizz-sticks, beaters, bowls) and line them up on the counter before they start disappearing .

Don't forget to turn on the oven before you start mixing if your recipe needs baking.

Even Super-Chefs try to cover-up. Put on an apron first.

Following the recipe exactly (at least the first time round) usually makes things tastier and more likely to turn out right.

Greasing a baking tin is done in a second if you use a piece of the butter wrapping.

Holding a measuring cup in the air only confuses the measurement, so always put it down on a flat surface to read.

If you still think in ounces, measure butter without scales (and convert it to grams) like this:

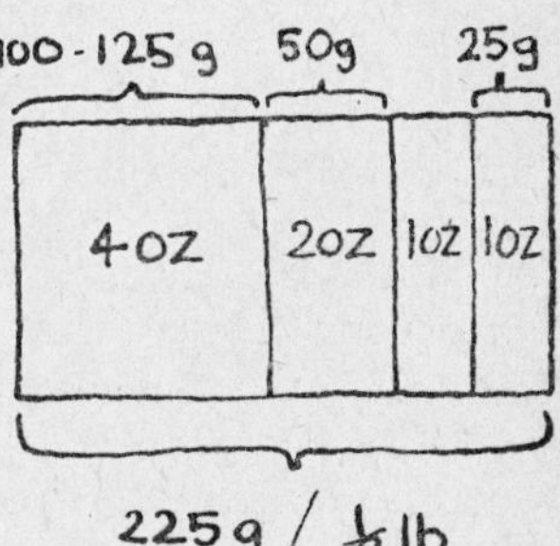

Just before you finish mixing, quickly read through the recipe to make sure you haven't left anything out.

Knowing that

1 oz sugar $=1\frac{1}{2}$ level tbsp$=$25 grams$=\frac{1}{8}$ cup (American)
1 oz flour $=2$ level tbsp$=$25 grams$=\frac{1}{4}$ cup (American)
1 oz butter$=2$ level tbsp$=$25 grams$=\frac{1}{8}$ cup (American)
1 oz raisins$=2$ level tbsp$=$25 grams$=\frac{1}{6}$ cup (American)

saves the day when you are missing either scales or measuring spoons.

Leave the sink full of hot soapy water while you are cooking so that you can put all used spoons and bowls straight in. Saves space and cuts washing-up time in half!

Milk comes in three different disguises:

used for most recipes

these two tinned varieties have most of the water taken out and are very thick. Use them in sweets and puddings.

Nuts can be chopped without a knife if you crush them (still in their bag) with a rolling pin or pound them with a small hammer or the end of a rolling pin.

Only a few centimetres but they can make a big difference to your baking. Always try to use exactly the size of baking tin suggested in the recipe.

Putting on oven gloves every time you take a hot pot off the stove or a pan out of the oven will make screams, curses and burned fingers a thing of the past.

Quick way to stir a liquid into a dry mixture is to make a 'well' or hole in the centre of the dry ingredients, pour liquid in, and then carefully stir round and round from the centre until it is all mixed in.

Remember to turn out cakes, breads and biscuits on to a wire rack to cool. They will get soggy if you leave them in the tin.

Sugar comes in a feast of shapes and sizes to suit different recipes.

Treacle and golden syrup are easier to measure if you dip the measuring spoon into hot water first. Then they glide right off the spoon.

Unless you prefer your pots burned and your brews boiled over, never leave anything on the stove unwatched.

Very hard brown sugar can be softened by putting it in a bowl in the oven (low heat) for a few minutes. If you put a slice of apple in the brown sugar package, you won't have this problem – it will never go hard.

Wooden spoons are whizz-sticks when it comes to creaming and stirring things in hot cauldrons, pots and pans. They will never burn your fingers, though a metal one might.

Xtra points for remembering to sift flour before you measure it. Whizz-Trick: Pour flour through a sieve on to the scales.

Yolks and whites are easily separated this way:

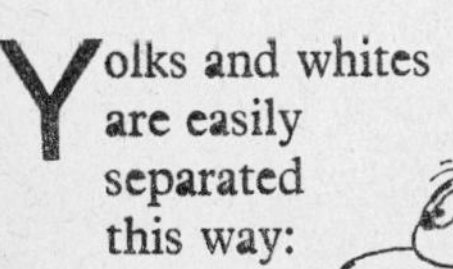

Zoom through the washing-up and whistle round the counters with a damp cloth and you will be the most popular Kitchen Wizard ever.

A MUNCHKIN BRUNCH

FLYING MONKEY MUFFINS

*

CRUNCHY-BRUNCHY

*

YELLOW BRICK BREAD

*

SMUNCHKINS

*

BLACKBERRY WITCHES

*

HONEY BUTTER

*

HOB-NOGGIN

A Munchkin Brunch

You can munch, you can crunch, you can lunch but don't say b-r-u-n-c-h in the Land of Oz. For if you happen to be in the East, the Munchkins will find you and insist upon BRUNCH! And this, as Dorothy discovered, is not a thing to be eaten lightly. Though part breakfast and part lunch, the Munchkins like eating it any time of day. This makes it easy for them to declare, whenever you arrive, that it must be time for Brunch. They won't mind sharing it with you in the least. In an instant, you will have a glass of Hob-Noggin in one hand and a double helping of Smunchkins with Honey Butter in the other.

Thanks to Dorothy, it is no longer necessary to kill a witch or arrive by cyclone to be entitled to a Munchkin Brunch. It just takes a few lessons from the Wizard himself . . .

Flying Monkey Muffins

Long ago in the Land of Oz, there was a magic golden cap which granted three wishes to the wearer. These wishes were carried out by a strange band of Flying Monkeys. Though the cap has been lost and the Monkeys have not been seen for years, the Munchkins keep dreaming up ways of enticing them back.

These muffins, dressed up to look like Flying Monkeys, are one of their favourite snacks. There is a certain magic about them, as you will see, for they *do* fly, especially off plates. Before you know it, your only wish will be for a few more Monkey Muffins.

SECRET INGREDIENTS

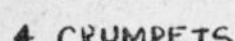

MAGIC FORMULA

1 *Grill both sides of* —— 4 crumpets
until well-toasted.

2 *Butter the top of each one*
then spread with —— peanut butter

3 *Grill until crispy* —— 8 bacon rashers
then drain on paper towelling.

4 *Crumble* 1 *bacon rasher on top of each crumpet. Cut remaining rashers in half and put* 2 *halves for wings on each crumpet. Use individual peanuts for the ears and tail.*

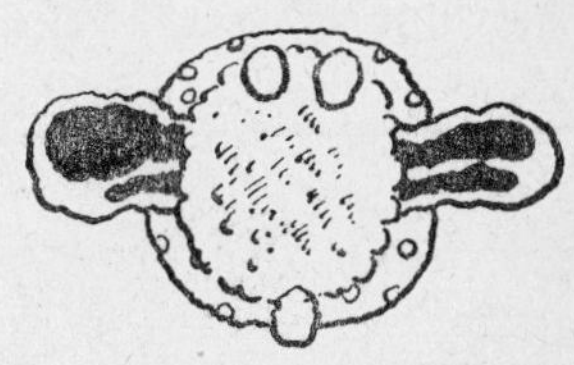

5 *Put Flying Monkeys on a baking tray and toast under the grill until the peanut butter is bubbling. Serve at once.*

WHIZZ TRICK

If you can't find crumpets or muffins, use large round rolls or baps instead.

Crunchy-Brunchy

Besides brunching, the Munchkins also like crunching, and anything else that sounds as good as it looks. It is impossible to eat Crunchy-Brunchy quietly and that's why they like it so much . With a supply of fruit, nuts and oats you can sample it yourself and find out what all the noise is about.

SECRET INGREDIENTS

MAGIC FORMULA

1 *Pre-heat oven to* 450°F (*Gas Mark* 8) 230°C

2 *Grease a baking tray.*

3 *Melt together in large saucepan over low heat and stir with whizz-stick until sugar is dissolved.* ——	50g butter 4 tbsp brown sugar 2 tbsp honey
4 *Add and mix thoroughly* ——	225g rolled oats 100g raisins 50g hazelnuts (optional)

5 *Pour mixture into greased baking tray and bake on top shelf of the oven until well-browned. Take the tray out and leave it to cool.*

6 *Crumble the Crunchy-Brunchy into small pieces with your hands and store in a tightly closed tin or plastic bag.*

7 *Serve in a bowl with lots of cold milk or eat it straight from the tin as a snack.*

WHIZZ TRICK

For a more colourful Crunchy-Brunchy, add slices of fresh fruit like apples, peaches, bananas, and serve with cold milk or yoghurt.

Yellow Brick Bread

To celebrate the opening of The Yellow Brick Road, all the Munchkin bakeries brought out their own versions of Yellow Brick Bread. Most of these tasted too much like real bricks and were quickly taken off the market. But one recipe was a great success and is still eaten by Munchkins today. No Brunch would be complete without it.

SECRET INGREDIENTS

MAGIC FORMULA

1 *Pre-heat oven to* 350°F (*Gas Mark* 4) 180°C	
2 *Grease a* 23cm *loaf tin*	
3 *Mash together in large bowl until very mushy*	3 ripe bananas
4 *Beat until light (the colour of custard) and add to bananas*	2 eggs
5 *Stir in*	25g melted butter ½ tsp vanilla
6 *Sift on to scales then sift together into banana mixture and blend in well.*	225g plain flour 175g sugar 1 tsp baking soda 1 tsp salt
7 *Add and mix in well* *Pour mixture into greased loaf tin.*	50g chopped walnuts

8 *Bake for* 1 *hour or until done (use the toothpick test).*

9 *Take out of the tin and cool on wire rack. Serve warm or cold, sliced and buttered.*

To store: wrap in cling-film and keep in a tin or bread box.

WHIZZ TRICK

Mashing bananas is much easier if you use a potato masher rather than a fork.

Smunchkins

'So good to munch,' was how Smunchkins originally began. But they were so popular that no one's mouth was empty long enough to say all this and soon all anyone managed to blurt out was 'smunchkin'. It also saved valuable time because there isn't a moment to lose when these cinnamon morsels appear. They taste best straight out of the oven with a little butter melting on top. The longer you leave them, the colder and less smunchkin they become. This provides an excellent excuse, or so the Munchkins claim, to hold a Brunch party immediately.

SECRET INGREDIENTS

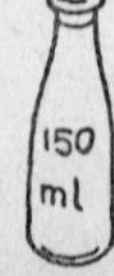

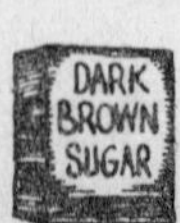

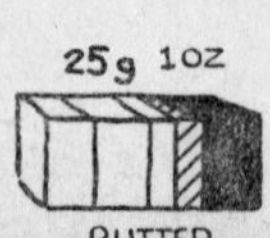

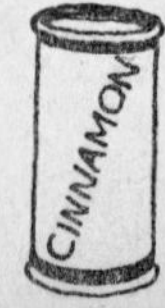

MAGIC FORMULA

1	*Pre-heat oven to* 425°F (*Gas Mark* 7)|220°C	
2	*Grease* 12 *patty tins*	
3	*Sift on to scales then sift together into mixing bowl.*	225g self-raising flour pinch of salt
4	*Break into small pieces then rub into flour mixture.*	50g butter
5	*Make a well in the dry ingredients, then carefully pour in and blend in with round-topped knife.*	150ml milk
6	*Turn dough out on to a lightly floured counter and knead gently for* 30 *seconds or until smooth.*	
7	*Dust a rolling pin with flour and roll dough into an oblong shape about* 30cm × 18cm *and* ½cm *thick.*	

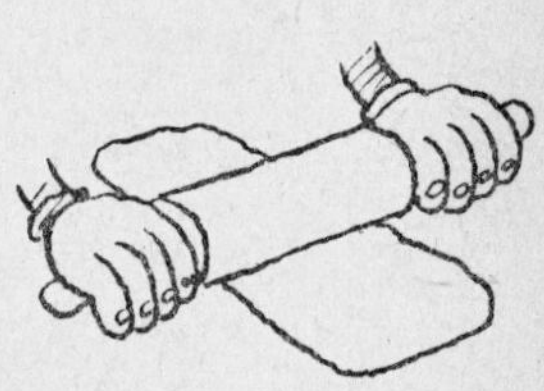

FILLING

8	*Spread dough evenly with*	25 g soft butter
9	*Mix together in small bowl and sprinkle over dough. Then, using the back of a spoon press it firmly into butter.*	50g brown sugar, sifted 1 tsp cinnamon
10	*Sprinkle on top of the butter/sugar mixture*	75g raisins or currants
11	*Roll dough up widthwise like a swiss roll and then cut into slices* 2.5cm *thick and place in patty tins.*	
12	*Press slices down slightly to fit patty tins and sprinkle with any remaining sugar and cinnamon mixture.*	
13	*Bake in centre of oven* 10–12 *minutes or until lightly browned. Serve hot with dollops of butter on top.*	

Blackberry Witches

The only thing that could spoil a Munchkin Brunch was the arrival of the Wicked Witch of the East. With one swoop of her broom, she would upset the Noggin, crush the Smunchkins and drop spiders in the Honey Butter. No one felt like brunching when she was around. You can imagine the cheers, then, when Dorothy's house landed on her, leaving nothing but a pair of silver shoes!

Just to remind themselves how lucky they are to be rid of this wicked woman, the Munchkins make a point of eating Blackberry Witch pancakes every other Friday. These look remarkably like a melted witch with bits of blackberry clothing dotted here and there.

SECRET INGREDIENTS

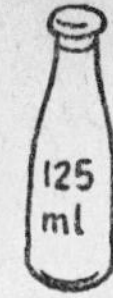

MAGIC FORMULA

1 *Sift on to scales* ——— *then sift together into a mixing bowl.*	125g plain flour large pinch salt
2 *Make a well in the flour mixture then carefully stir in* ———	1 egg mixed with 50ml milk
3 *Then gradually beat in* ———	75ml milk
4 *Put into a small bowl and stir* ——— *until sugar is dissolved*	1 small tin blackberries (*with juice*) 3½ tbsp sugar

5 *Gradually blend blackberries and juice,* 1 *tbsp at a time, into the egg batter.*

6 *Put just enough cooking oil into a frying pan to cover the bottom and put on medium heat.*

7 *Pour batter into a jug and when the oil starts to smell, pour small amounts of batter into the frying pan.*

8 *Turn once and when golden brown on both sides, lift the Witches out of the frying pan with a fish slice and put on a plate in the oven* (300°F, *Gas Mark* 2) 150°C *to keep warm until serving.*

9 *Sprinkle with caster sugar and lemon juice or spread with Honey Butter.*

WHIZZ TRICK

If you can't find blackberries, don't despair. Use the same quantity of another canned fruit to make Raspberry, Peach or even Bilberry Witches.

Honey Butter

Munchkins are rather fond of Blackberry Witches with Honey Butter. This they make in large quantities so there is never any danger of running out. Occasionally, when they fancy a Witch with a bit more spice to it, they whistle up a bowl or two of Cinnamon Honey Butter. And for times when a really first-rate Honey Butter is in order, they will get out the beater and whip up some Creamy Honey Butter. But then, of course, if it is an extra special occasion they are just as likely to come up with a little Maple Honey Butter.

SECRET INGREDIENTS

MAGIC FORMULA

1 *In a small bowl, use a whisk to whip until light and fluffy* —— 50g soft butter

2 *Then whisk in gradually, ½ tbsp at a time, and whip until smooth and shiny.* —— 4 level tbsp honey

CINNAMON HONEY BUTTER

3 *Whisk in* —— 1 heaped tsp cinnamon

CREAMY HONEY BUTTER

3 *Whisk in* —— 3 tbsp sifted icing sugar

Very slowly, 1 *tsp at a time, whisk in* —— 1 tbsp single cream

MAPLE HONEY BUTTER

3 *Whisk in gradually,* ½ *tsp at a time, until well-blended.* —— 2 tsp maple syrup

Put into a tightly covered container and keep in the refrigerator. Leave at room temperature for 15 minutes before using. Delicious on toast and Witches.

Hob-Noggin

The Munchkins, unlike that Humbug, the Wizard of Oz, love company and there isn't anything they like better than a good hobnob with friends. To make hobnobbing better than ever, they have invented a special drink to go with it. This is an unusual type of noggin which can be whisked at a moment's notice and even the smallest Munchkin can make it. To give it an extra nip, they usually add a little orange juice, or they might even tint it purple with a spoonful of blackcurrant syrup. Whatever the colour, the Munchkins find it irresistible.

SECRET INGREDIENTS

MAGIC FORMULA

1 *In large mixing bowl, beat with rotary or electric beater until thick.*	1 egg 1 dessertspoon honey pinch salt
2 *Beat in gradually*	225ml cold milk 50ml orange juice ½ tsp vanilla
3 *Pour into a large jug, add a few ice cubes if you have them, and serve straight away.*	
4 *Top each glass of Hob-noggin with a sprinkling of*	ground nutmeg

Keep any left-over Noggin in the refrigerator and whip it up quickly before serving again.

WHIZZ TRICK

Put left-over Hob-Noggin into a large clean coffee jar and screw the top on tightly. To make it frothy again, just shake back and forth vigorously (using both hands) for a minute before serving.

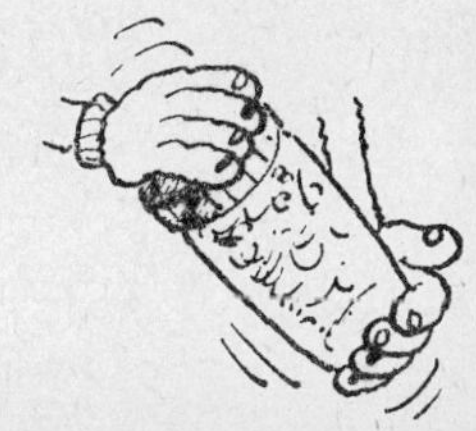

LUNCH IN LILLIPUT

FRUIT ARROWS

*

IMPERIAL PIZZAS

*

TRIPLE GLUMGLUFFS

*

EMPRESS TARTS

*

CREAM SNIPPETS

*

FLIMNAP'S FOLLY

*

LILLIPUT PALACE

Lunch in Lilliput

When Gulliver was washed up on the beach of Lilliput he terrified the inhabitants. No wonder. He was twelve times their size! If they stood on tiptoe they could just see over his kneecap and with a boost, a few brave ones crawled up on his chest. Their first reaction was to tie this giant to the ground before he could do any damage. If he took up that much space lying down, imagine what would happen if he stood up. With ladders and lorry-loads of rope, they finally tied him down and then just for good measure bombarded him with arrows. It took some time for Gulliver to convince them that he hadn't the slightest intention of waging war against them. They did at last untie him, on condition that he bellow loudly before every move so that the natives would not be crushed underfoot.

For the nation's safety, they insisted he live in a deserted temple outside the city gates, but then did their best to make him feel at home. An imperial commission was set up specially by the Emperor of Lilliput to see that the Man-Mountain was well looked after. By order of His Majesty, every village within 900 yards was obliged to deliver meat, fruit and wine to Gulliver's doorstep every morning. Three hundred cooks prepared his food while 600 Lilliputians were kept busy at his domestic chores. Six of His Majesty's scholars taught him the language of Lilliput and over 300 tailors worked on a suit of clothes.

If you were suddenly to shrink to a size of barely six inches, it might be helpful to know what a Lilliputian lunch tastes like.

Fruit Arrows

It wasn't long before the Lilliputians realized that the arrows they were shooting at Gulliver were hurting them more than him. They wisely decided to save their strength and bring him under control by other means. A potion slipped into his drink sent him straight to sleep and spared them any further trouble. However, they discovered some time later that their arrows could serve a more useful purpose. Quite by accident they found that they were an excellent way of transporting food to Gulliver's mouth. In this way they could stuff several sheep, a whole cheese and several pieces of fruit on one arrow and give Gulliver quite a decent mouthful.

SECRET INGREDIENTS

MAGIC FORMULA

1 *Drain the pineapple chunks, putting the juice in a separate container. Dice the cheese into* 2cm *squares. Cut each piece of ham in four lengthwise.*

2 *Put a square of cheese at one end of each ham slice and roll up tightly to the other end.*

3 *On each toothpick, thread a pineapple chunk, a piece of rolled up ham and cheese, and then another pineapple chunk.*

ARROW GLAZE

4 *Mix together in small saucepan and stir over low heat until sugar is dissolved. Then let mixture boil gently, stirring occasionally, until thick and syrupy.* ——— 2 tbsp pineapple juice
2 tbsp water
2 tbsp brown sugar
1 heaped tbsp honey

5 *Place the arrows close together on a baking tray and spoon arrow glaze over each one.*

6 *Pop the arrows under the grill for about 5 minutes, turning once and basting with the juices, until the ham is slightly browned. Serve at once.*

WHIZZ TRICK

To make your arrows look really authentic, serve them from a red apple target. Wash and polish a large red apple, stand it on a plate and then stick the arrows all around the base.

Imperial Pizzas

This dish was the Emperor's favourite. It was made with a unique sauce which caused quite a sensation the first time it was served at one of the Emperor's supper parties. This sauce was spread on a special crust which had been buttered and covered with cheese. To prevent anyone discovering the secret ingredients of the sauce, the chef then topped it with mushrooms or slices of cooked sausage.

One of these pizzas provided an ample supper for His Majesty, the Empress and the royal Princes. But Gulliver could not stop at one and frequently ate half a dozen at one sitting.

SECRET INGREDIENTS

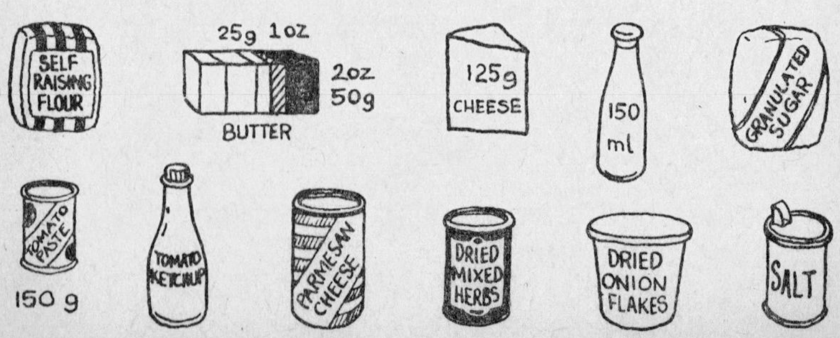

MAGIC FORMULA

1 *Pre-heat oven to* 450°F (*Gas Mark* 8) 230°C

2 *Grease a baking tray*

3 *Sift on to scales* ——— 225g self-raising flour
then sift together into mixing bowl. ½ tsp salt

4 *Cut into small pieces*
then rub in ——— 50g butter

5 *Pour in* ——— 150ml milk
and blend in with round-topped knife.

6 *Turn dough out on to lightly floured counter and knead gently for half a minute or until smooth.*

7 *Roll out until* ½cm *thick. Put small saucer down on the dough and cut round it to make the pizza bases. Place each one on the baking tray, pressing it down flat with your fingers and turning all the edges up high enough* (*about* 2cm) *to keep sauce from escaping.*

8 *Spread dough with small amount of soft butter and cover with* ——— cheese, sliced (cut to fit the round) or grated

Then spread with pizza sauce.

PIZZA SAUCE

9 *Mix together in a small bowl* ———
1 small tin tomato paste
2 tbsp tomato ketchup
2 tbsp grated Parmesan cheese
2 tbsp water
1 tbsp sugar
2 tsp mixed herbs
1 tsp dried onion flakes

10 *If you like, this can be topped with sliced mushrooms, sausages or frankfurters in true Lilliput style.*

11 *Bake pizzas just above centre of oven for approximately* 20 *minutes. Serve hot or cold.*

Triple Glumgluffs

The Lilliputians were excellent mathematicians and everything was measured down to the last glumgluff (which is about an inch). Gulliver, doing his best to understand their mathematics, tried to think in terms of glumgluffs rather than inches. While doing this, he was struck by the fact that each large meat loaf they brought him for lunch was exactly the size of three glumgluffs. So he persisted in calling these loaves Triple Glumgluffs. This naturally annoyed the cooks who felt it a very undignified name for such a tempting dish but Gulliver refused to give up his mathematics lesson and Glumgluffs stayed on the menu.

SECRET INGREDIENTS

MAGIC FORMULA

1 *Pre-heat oven to* 425°F (*Gas Mark* 7) 220°C

2 *Mix together with a fork in large bowl* — 450g lean minced beef
1 egg
1 slice bread, torn into pieces
1 tbsp dried onion flakes
1 tsp salt
½ tsp pepper

3 *With your hands (wash first!) shape meat mixture into small loaves and place on a rack in a roasting pan.*

4 *In a small bowl, mix together well* —— 3 tbsp tomato ketchup
1 heaped tbsp brown sugar
1 tbsp water
1 tbsp honey
1 tbsp vinegar
½ tbsp mild mustard
1 tsp Worcestershire sauce

5 *With a knife, spread the sauce over each glumgluff, covering top and sides well.*

6 *Bake in the oven on the middle or top shelf for* 15–20 *minutes (or until cooked through). Serve hot or cold.*

Empress Tarts

The Empress of Lilliput frequently paid Gulliver social calls, accompanied by her ladies-in-waiting. On these occasions she used to bring a few titbits from the Palace kitchens. These tarts were her undoing and she would often have a small corner of one to go with her tea, while Gulliver polished off the rest of it in one mouthful.

SECRET INGREDIENTS

MAGIC FORMULA

1 *Pre-heat oven to* 350°F (*Gas Mark* 4) 180°C

2 *Grease lightly* 9 *patty tins and press a cake case firmly into each one.*

3 *Put into a plastic bag, tie tightly, and crush to fine crumbs with rolling pin.*	8 digestive biscuits
4 *Melt together in a small saucepan over low heat, stirring with a whizz-stick until sugar is dissolved.*	5 level tbsp butter 2 tbsp sugar

5 *Take off the heat and blend in biscuit crumbs. Then line each cake case with mixture by pressing crumbs firmly into the bottom and sides with the back of a teaspoon.*

6 *Put the patty tins into the refrigerator and leave to chill for at least* 15 *minutes.*

LEMON FILLING

7 *Mix together in small bowl then put to one side.*	2 egg yolks 6 tbsp lemon curd

MERINGUE

8 *Beat until standing in soft peaks*	2 egg whites
Beat in (1 *tbsp at a time*) *and continue beating until stiff and glossy.*	100g sugar

9 *Take patty tins out of the refrigerator and fill each cake case* $\frac{2}{3}$ *full with lemon mixture.*

10 *Then heap meringue on the tarts, making sure it seals in the lemon filling by covering all the edges.*

11 *Bake in the middle of the oven for* 10 *minutes or until the meringue is lightly browned.*

12 *Take out of the oven and leave to set for a few hours. Store in the refrigerator.*

Cream Snippets

Feeling slightly guilty at keeping so many chefs busy, Gulliver decided one day to cook something for them. He gave the Lilliput School of Cookery a morning demonstration and found to his surprise that they had never come across Cream Snippets before. By the end of the day everyone was making Snippets and in no time at all they became the fashionable thing to serve at teas and buffet lunches.

They became even better known when Lilliput next went to war with Blefescu. Someone accidentally discovered that Cream Snippets fitted perfectly into the cannons and made excellent cannonballs. When the Blefescuans landed on the beaches, they were hit by a barrage of Snippets and completely drowned in whipped cream!

Cream Snippets don't seem to have the same effect on enemies these days, as they only come back for more.

SECRET INGREDIENTS

MAGIC FORMULA

1 *Pre-heat oven to* 400°F (*Gas Mark* 6) 200°C

2 *Grease a baking tray*

3 *Mix together in a saucepan and bring to the boil.*	150ml water 50g butter
4 *Take off the heat and add all at once Stir mixture vigorously until it leaves the sides of the pan and forms a ball in the centre.*	75g plain flour, sifted pinch salt
5 *Add* 1 *at a time beating well with a whizz-stick after each addition. Continue beating until mixture is smooth and shiny.*	2 eggs, unbeaten

6 *Drop mixture by rounded tablespoonfuls,* 5cm *apart, on to baking tray. Bake on middle shelf in the oven for at least* 30 *minutes. Turn the heat off and leave for another ten minutes.*

7 *Take the snippets out and cool on a wire rack.*

ICING

8 *Melt in a saucepan over gentle heat and stir with whizz-stick until sugar is dissolved.*	50g butter 50g brown sugar
9 *Take off the heat and stir in until well blended.*	25ml milk
10 *Then stir in and beat with whizz-stick until smooth.*	75g icing sugar, sifted ½tsp vanilla
11 *Slice snippets horizontally and remove any wet dough in the centre.*	
12 *Fill bottom halves with dollops of and swirl the tops round quickly in the icing. If you find the icing too runny, leave to cool slightly; if too thick, add more milk. Then put the* 2 *halves together again. Eat at once or freeze* 1–2 *hours in freezing compartment.*	vanilla ice-cream or double cream (whipped stiff; add sugar to taste)

Flimnap's Folly

Flimnap was the disagreeable Treasurer of Lilliput. He disliked Gulliver from the start and did his best to make things difficult for him. When it was rumoured that his wife was secretly fond of Gulliver, Flimnap was furious and tried twice as hard to get him beheaded, imprisoned or at least thrown out of the country. He was very prim and proper, priding himself on his ability to do sums so well in his head. Flimnap's only weakness was a special drink made by his wife. It was a cider punch cooked with spices and fruits and the smell of this wafting through the kitchen made him feel quite weak at the knees. He was unable to stop at one glass and after three or four could be found stretched across the table, snoring loudly. He would be full of apologies when he awoke, but still insist on being the first to try the next batch!

The recipe below is a version of Flimnap's Folly and unless you are very foolish and drink too much of it, you should not suffer Flimnap's fate.

SECRET INGREDIENTS

LEMON

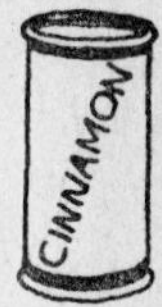

MAGIC FORMULA

1 *Wash thoroughly and slice* ———— 2 apples
(no need to core or peel them) 2 oranges

2 *Stick into the orange skins* ———— 8 cloves

3 *Put in a saucepan with* ———— 950ml sweet cider
juice of 1 lemon
4 tbsp brown sugar
1 tsp cinnamon
1 tsp mixed spice

5 *Bring to the boil, then cover and simmer for* 15 *minutes.*

6 *Pour through a sieve into mugs and serve at once.*

WHIZZ TRICK

For a more festive Flimnap's Folly, give each glass a snow cap of ice-cream or whipped cream.

Lilliput Palace

The Emperor and Empress were most anxious that Gulliver should come to the Palace and have a good look around the state apartments. This was, of course, impossible because of his size. One step into the courtyard and he would have crushed all His Majesty's prize-winning rose bushes. But if Gulliver lay down outside the Palace on his side he could get quite a good view into the apartments on the second floor. When he arrived at tea-time, the Emperor and Empress sat on the window sill chatting, while a huge hoist was rigged up to hold a giant cup of tea and tray of cakes for Gulliver. This worked out quite well but Gulliver did find it slightly uncomfortable and tried to restrict these side visits to half an hour.

Because of its small size, you can build Lilliput Palace without the help of an architect. This model gives just the basic design so that you can add all your own innovations.

SECRET INGREDIENTS

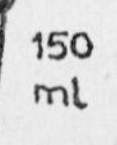

OR WHIPPING CREAM

MAGIC FORMULA

1 *Turn oven to its lowest setting* (275°F *or Gas Mark* 1) 140°C

2 *Cover* 3 *baking trays with foil or heavy brown paper.*

3 *Beat until standing in soft peaks* ——— 4 egg whites
Beat in (1 *tbsp at a time*) ——— 225g sugar
and continue beating until stiff and glossy.

4 *Using* 2 *teaspoons, drop circles of this meringue on to the baking trays. Make* 8 *large circles* (*about* 7 cm *across*) *on the* 1*st tray,* 8 *medium* (*about* 6cm *across*) *on the* 2*nd,* 8 *small* (*about* 5cm) *on the* 3*rd.*

5 *Bake on lowest shelves of the oven for* 1½ *hours.*

6 *Then turn off the oven and leave until the oven is quite cold (best to leave them overnight). Don't open the oven door until you take them out.*

7 *Carefully peel off the foil or paper and put the circles on three different plates, according to size.*

8 *Whip until thick and standing in stiff peaks* ——— 150ml double cream
Fold in with metal spoon ——— 1 tbsp caster sugar

9 *Cover a small tray or breadboard with foil and use it as a base for the Palace. Carefully slice off 'peaks' of the* 8 *large and medium circles. Make a square with the* 8 *largest meringue circles. Put a dollop of whipped cream in the centre of each one, then put a slightly smaller circle on top. Build up the castle walls like this, saving the small peaked circles for the turrets and the top layer of the side walls. Crumble left over 'peaks' to fill the courtyard in the centre.* 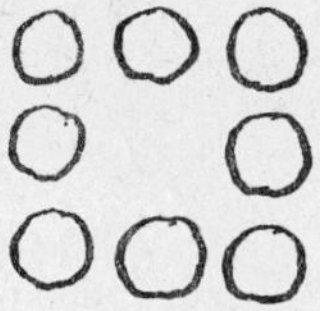 
P.S. If you use 275ml *cream* (*and* 1 *more tbsp sugar*) *you will have enough to fill in the walls with cream as well.*

A HUCKLEBERRY FINN RAFT PICNIC

BAREFOOT BREAD

*

HICKORY CHICKEN

*

HOBO ROLL-UPS

*

HUCKLEBERRY BUCKLE

*

PLAYIN' HOOKEY COOKIES
(Tom's Favourite)

*

PENUCKLE

*

BY JINGO! JUICE

A Huckleberry Finn Raft Picnic

As far as Huckleberry Finn was concerned, there wasn't anything nicer than a raft picnic. Tom Sawyer agreed, especially if you managed to slip out of school without being seen, raid Aunt Polly's larder without being caught and get down to the river without it raining!

No-one knows *exactly* what a raft picnic is because it has always been a top Finn-Sawyer secret. But it seems that it doesn't necessarily need to take place on a raft or on any boat at all. All you need is one or two rather special ingredients . .

Barefoot Bread

Tom and Huck were none too partial to wearing shoes, so they took them off at the first opportunity. Huck took off his at the beginning of March and put them back on at the end of October. They didn't care much for 'fancy fixins' either and packing up for a picnic meant taking the easiest things possible. Cornmeal was the best to carry because it could be stuffed straight into pockets and corn pone (Barefoot Bread) was so simple to make that even Tom and Huck could manage it.

You can make it in a frying pan over an open fire or in the oven, depending on your picnic site.

SECRET INGREDIENTS

MAGIC FORMULA

1 *Pre-heat oven to* 425°F (*Gas Mark* 7) 220°C

2 *Grease* 23cm *square tin with high sides.*

3 *Sift on to scales* —— 125g plain flour
then sift together into large bowl.
125g cornmeal
75g sugar
3 tsp baking powder
1 tsp salt

4 *Melt in small saucepan over low heat* —— 50g butter

5 *In a small bowl, beat lightly* —— 1 egg

6 *Pour melted butter and beaten egg into flour mixture (don't forget to make a 'well' in the flour first) with* —— 225ml milk
Mix only until flour is blended in (don't beat).

7 *Pour batter into greased tin and bake on middle shelf in the oven for* 20–25 *minutes or until done (use toothpick test).*

8 *Serve piping hot, sliced and spread with butter (and jam, if you like).*

WHIZZ TRICK

To make Skillet Bread, grease a large frying pan well and put over a very low heat to warm until you are ready to use it. When the batter is ready, pour it in and cover with a lid. Cook over a low heat for about 30 minutes (or until done – use the toothpick test).

Hickory Chicken

As raft picnics always tended to be rather spur of the moment, planning for them was practically impossible. Tom did try occasionally, if he felt he was on the brink of one, to store up a few provisions beforehand. But this was never very successful. Either Sid, his room-mate, would discover his hideaway and spill the beans to Aunt Polly, or he would suddenly be overcome by Acute Starvation in the middle of the night and forced to eat the lot.

So, in the end, he had to make a last-minute raid on Aunt Polly's larder for a few pocket-sized items. These never amounted to much, except on one memorable occasion when he squeezed four pieces of chicken into his back pocket. These were received with great relish by Huck, who rolled them in melted butter and fried them instantly over the fire.

SECRET INGREDIENTS

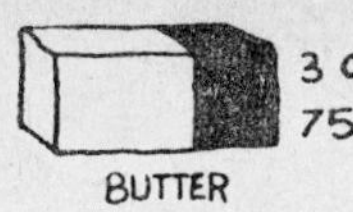

MAGIC FORMULA

1 *Pre-heat oven to* 400°F (*Gas Mark* 6) 200°C

2 *Pour into a plastic bag tie tightly and crush to crumbs with rolling pin.* —— 50g potato crisps

3 *Melt in small frying pan* —— 75g butter

4 *Roll both sides of chicken pieces in melted butter, then drop one at a time into bag with crisp crumbs. Holding the bag tightly with one hand, shake well until the chicken is well covered in crumbs.*

5 *Place the chicken in a baking tin, skin side up. When all the chicken pieces are ready to go in the oven, pour the rest of the melted butter and crumbs over them. Shake a little salt, pepper and paprika over each piece.*

6 *Bake for* 1 *hour, basting occasionally with juices in tin. Serve hot or cold.*

WHIZZ TRICK

For a more unusual flavour, vary the type of potato crisp you use. Try bacon, onion or cheese and notice the difference in taste.

Hobo Roll-Ups

Huck was the envy of all the other boys because no one could make him go to church, or wash behind his ears. He swam when it suited him and didn't care a hoot about school. His trousers, always rolled up to the knee, were the perfect length for fishing and fence-climbing. 'T'aint fair, t'aint right,' Tom used to say, because when he and the others tried to follow Huck's glorious example all they got was a good thrashing! Their only chance to play hobo with Huck was to escape down the river for a raft picnic.

These sandwiches, which seemed to turn up on every picnic, looked so much like Huck's trousers that they were always called Hobo Roll-ups.

SECRET INGREDIENTS

MAGIC FORMULA

1 *Cut crusts off and toast both sides of* ——— 4 slices of bread

2 *Butter one side of each slice and cover with* ——— 1 slice cheese
1 slice ham (on top)

3 *Put on a baking tray and grill until the ham is slightly browned and the cheese is bubbling underneath.*

4 *Leave to cool for a few minutes then roll each one up like a swiss roll. Stick a toothpick through the centre to keep it from falling apart.*

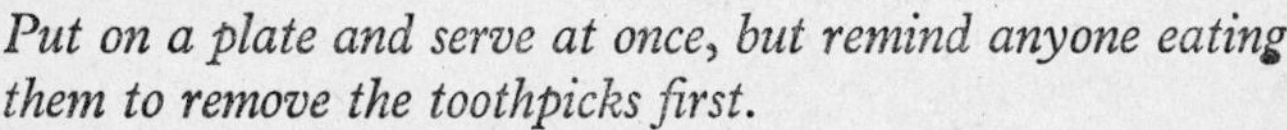

Put on a plate and serve at once, but remind anyone eating them to remove the toothpicks first.

WHIZZ TRICK

Huck and Tom used the crusts as bait for fishing but you might prefer to put them in a tin and use them later to make bread-crumbs (delicious on top of Mountain Soup or Possum Pie).

Huckleberry Buckle

If there was one thing Huck used to get a hankering for it was huckleberries. And if he couldn't find huckleberries, then blueberries would do. He could eat them until he was blue in the face and never felt right about leaving a few on the bush. But then the clever Widow Douglas convinced him that it wasn't necessary to eat them all at one sitting. If he found a safe place to hide them, he could have a blueberry tuck-in for days. She claimed the safest place was in a lump of dough. If it hadn't tasted so good straight out of the oven Huck would never have believed her. Best of all it was so 'gol durned easy' that Huck could make it himself in a jiffy. Good thing too that the longer you kept it the better it tasted!

P.S. No one knows to this day how it got the Buckle part of its name. That was Huck's own secret.

SECRET INGREDIENTS

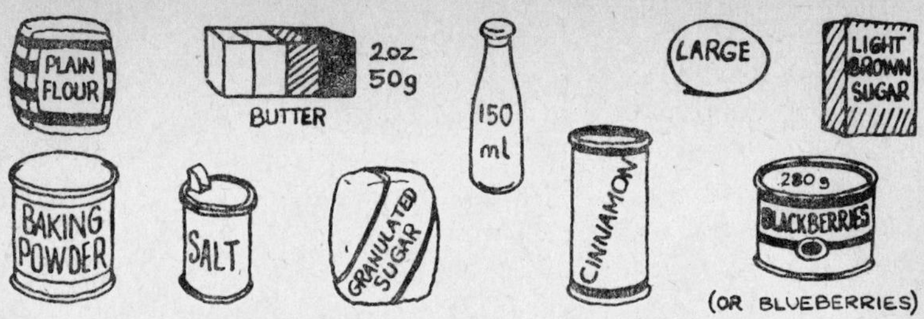

MAGIC FORMULA

1 *Pre-heat oven to* 350°F (*Gas Mark* 4) 180°C

2 *Grease a* 23cm *square tin and line with greaseproof paper. Grease again.*

3 ***Sift** on to scales* ——— *then sift together into large bowl.*	250g plain flour 175g sugar 2½ tsp baking powder ¾ tsp salt
4 *Melt in a saucepan over low heat* ———	50g butter
5 *Make a well in the flour mixture and pour melted butter in with* ——— *Stir only enough to moisten dry ingredients.*	1 egg, beaten 150ml milk
6 *Carefully stir in* ——— *Pour mixture into greased tin.*	1 large tin of blackberries (drained of juice)

TOPPING

7 *Mix together in small bowl* ———	75g brown sugar 50g plain flour, sifted 1 tsp cinnamon
8 *Break into small pieces and rub in* ——— *Sprinkle evenly over batter in tin.*	50g cold butter

9 *Bake for one hour or until toothpick stuck in the centre comes out clean. Lift carefully out of tin holding on to the greaseproof paper and put on to wire rack. Serve hot or cold with butter. If you wrap it in cling-film and store in airtight container it will stay fresh for days.*

Playin' Hookey Cookies

(Tom's Favourite)

One whiff of these cookies baking in the oven and Tom just knew it was time for a picnic. There was nothing he could do to stop his feet going straight to the kitchen and before you could say Jack Robinson, he had hooked half a dozen from right under Aunt Polly's nose. They always tasted twice as good down by the river, even if he did have to share them occasionally with Huck. He never meant to play hookey* but a pocketful of these cookies made going to school impossible: one sniff of that peanutty smell and the whole class would demand their share!

* truant

SECRET INGREDIENTS

MAGIC FORMULA

1 *Pre-heat oven to* 350°F (*Gas Mark* 4) 180°C

2 *Lightly grease a baking tray*

3 *Cream together in large mixing bowl until light and fluffy.* —— 125g soft butter, 125g crunchy peanut butter

4 *Sift on to scales and add gradually to butter mixture.* —— 125g granulated sugar, 125g brown sugar

5 *With whizz-stick, beat in* —— 1 egg, ½ tsp vanilla

6 *Sift and add, mixing in well* —— 150g self-raising flour

7 *Flour hands lightly and roll dough into small balls (about the size of walnuts). Place on baking tray about* 5cm *apart. Flatten them with a floured fork.*

8 *Bake just above the centre of the oven for* 10–12 *minutes. Remove cookies from tray with palette knife and cool on wire rack.*

WHIZZ TRICK

For cookies with even more crunch, stir in 50g crushed or chopped peanuts to the dough when the flour has been blended in.

Penuckle

Tom reckoned he had a sweet tooth and Huck thought he had about six. The sweeter a thing was, the better they liked it; and better still, if it lasted a long time. Tom and Huck had a race once to see whose piece of Penuckle lasted the longest. Huck won as he still had a sliver of peanut left after a record five minutes. Perhaps you can beat this!

SECRET INGREDIENTS

MAGIC FORMULA

1 *Grease a large baking tray*

2 *Mix together in a heavy saucepan over medium heat. Stir until sugar is dissolved, then bring to the boil.* ——— 125g sugar, 125g golden syrup, 50ml water

3 *Stirring occasionally, boil until a small amount dropped into cold water forms hard, brittle threads.*

4 *Then add and mix well* ——— 100g unsalted peanuts

5 *Take off the heat and stir in quickly* ——— 1 tbsp butter, ½ tsp baking soda, ½ tsp vanilla

5 *Pour immediately on to greased baking tray. Leave in cool place to harden, then break into small pieces.*

6 *Store in the refrigerator or tightly covered tin.*

WHIZZ TRICK

To measure 125g golden syrup quickly, put the tin on the scales. Note its weight, then take out tablespoonfuls (about 3) until the scales read 125g less than that.

By Jingo! Juice

Tom had a few favourite expressions. One of them was 'Oh Geeminy', another was 'Aw, Shucks', but the best was 'By Jingo!' Whenever he and Huck were raft-picnicking, they used to concoct a special brew. They would pick fresh berries, mash them with sugar and add just about anything that was handy. The result was so scrumptious that the only words to describe it were 'By Jingo!', and so it was.

If you don't have fresh berries on hand, berry syrup is just as good. The recipe below uses blackcurrant syrup with mouth-watering results.

SECRET INGREDIENTS

MAGIC FORMULA

1 *Squeeze the juice of one of and cut the other into slices.*	2 oranges
2 *Mix together with in large jug.*	3 tbsp blackcurrant syrup 2 bottles ginger ale ice cubes

3 *Stir well and serve at once.*

If preparing beforehand, leave out the ice cubes and ginger ale until the last minute.

WHIZZ TRICK

Make up a tray of ice cubes, stirring 3 tbsp of blackcurrant syrup into the water. Freeze and add these currant cubes at the last moment to the drink.

You can also drop small pieces of the orange slices into the ice-cube sections before freezing to make them more colourful.

A BOSTON TEA PARTY

CHEESY TEA CHESTS

*

REBEL STACKS

*

BOSTON SPLITS

*

TOLLHOUSE COOKIES

*

HONEY MOHAWKS

*

HOPSCOTCH BROWNIES

*

LIBERTY PUNCH

A Boston Tea Party

Imagine a tea party where, instead of drinking tea, you threw it over your shoulder! If you had been in Boston Harbour on the night of December 16, 1773, this is just what you might have been doing. Disguised as a Red Indian with a few daubs of paint and a blanket tied around your waist, you would be heading down to Griffin's Wharf with a number of other 'Mohawks'. Shortly before six o'clock, just as it was getting dark, you would divide into three groups, each boarding one of the British ships moored there. With a cry of, 'Boston Harbour a teapot to-night!' you would then set about breaking open all the tea chests on the ship and heaving the tea overboard. This was a somewhat precarious task as it was low tide and the water, soon swollen with tea leaves, threatened at one point to swamp the ships' decks. Two hours later, the entire cargo (342 tea chests) would be lying at the bottom of the harbour. A good way to make iced tea, perhaps, but hardly the way to win favour with the British Government!

If you feel slightly rebellious and would like to demonstrate your protest in a more friendly way, why not organise your own Boston Tea Party? This modern version is such an improvement on the first that it is guaranteed to win friends, not lose them.

Cheesy Tea Chests

The three ships which lost their cargoes so abruptly that night had been docked in Boston Harbour for some time. The American colonists refused to let them unload as a protest against paying the tax on tea. While waiting for the British Government to remove this unpopular tax, they took great pleasure in making their own tea chests out of brown bread and secretly dumping them, either into their mouths or straight into a bowl of soup.

If you would like to taste these tea chests, you might prefer to give them a dry run first.

SECRET INGREDIENTS

OR

MAGIC FORMULA

1 *Soften with a fork in a small bowl* — 75g cream cheese

2 *Then whisk in gradually* — 2 dessertspoons of milk
1½ tsp sugar

3 *Stir in* — 4 tsp diced pineapple (well-drained)

4 *Butter one side of* — 8 slices brown bread

5 *Divide the slices into two piles of* 4. *Then stack them up, spreading*
the first layer with — cheese/pineapple mixture
the second layer with — jam or honey
the third layer with — cheese/pineapple mixture

5 *Top off each stack with a final slice placed butter side down.*

6 *Pressing down firmly* (*to push the layers together*), *trim the crusts off. Then cut each stack into four quarters.*

7 *Put the tea chests on a plate and chill until serving.*

Rebel Stacks

To discourage the British captains from unloading their ships, the Bostonians posted an armed guard on the docks to keep a 24-hour watch. To make the job of watchdog more appealing, the men were issued with a large sandwich when they went on duty. Stuffed with tomatoes and bacon it provided delicious ammunition against the long hours and cold winds. It soon became known as a Rebel Stack and was especially popular because it tasted good hot or cold.

One word of warning: if you are making these for a Boston Tea Party, don't taste one first or you will never be able to give the rest away.

SECRET INGREDIENTS

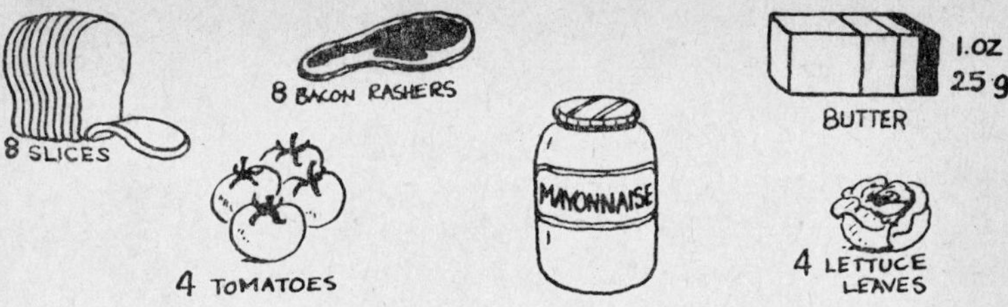

MAGIC FORMULA

1 *Grill until crispy* —— 8 bacon rashers
then drain on paper towelling.
Break each rasher in half.

2 *Wash and slice carefully* —— 4 tomatoes

3 *Toast on both sides* —— 8 slices of bread

4 *Spread one side of* 4 *slices with* —— butter
and one side of the other 4 *slices with* —— mayonnaise

5 *On top of all the mayonnaise-covered slices, put a few tomato slices,* 4 *bacon halves and a lettuce leaf.*

6 *Cover each one with a slice of toast (butter side down) and press down firmly.*

7 *Cut into quarters and serve immediately.*

WHIZZ TRICK

If you cut the bacon fat like this it won't curl up when you grill it.

Boston Splits

After meetings at the town hall, look-out postings and watchdog duty, there wasn't much time left for eating. But there was somehow always time for Boston Splits. These creamy egg sandwiches, easy to pocket and even easier to eat, turned up everywhere. There wasn't a family in Boston during this time that didn't have a supply of them made up and ready to go. A large plateful was kept inside the front door as emergency rations for anyone who had to rush out in a hurry.

Though Boston Splits are extremely filling, you'll find that one is never enough.

SECRET INGREDIENTS

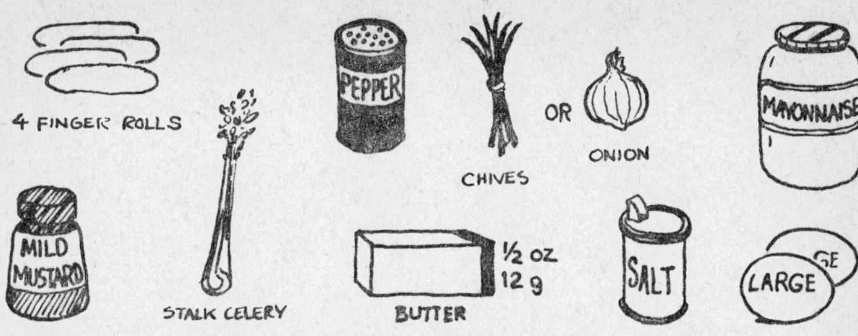

MAGIC FORMULA

1 *Cover with water in a small saucepan and bring to the boil* ——— 2 large eggs
Boil for 10 *minutes.*

2 *Put the eggs immediately under the cold water tap replacing hot water with cold. Leave the eggs to cool.*

3 *Peel the eggs and put into a medium bowl. Mash with a fork until the eggs look like bread crumbs.*

4 *Then stir in* ———
- 2 heaped tbsp finely chopped celery
- 2 tbsp mayonnaise
- 1 tbsp melted butter
- 1 tsp grated onion or chopped chives
- ½ tsp mild mustard
- salt and pepper to taste

5 *Slice open and butter* ——— 4 finger rolls
Fill with dollops of the egg mixture.

6 *Put on a plate and keep in the refrigerator until ready to serve.*

Tollhouse Cookies

The three captains, who were forbidden to unload their ships or leave the harbour, became increasingly annoyed as the weeks went by. Surrounded by tea, it was no wonder they resorted to drinking it in large quantities. As they spent a great deal of time at the Custom House, their cups of tea were often accompanied by special biscuits made by the custom officer's wife. Unlike anything they had ever tasted before, the captains soon re-named these Custom House, or Tollhouse, Cookies.

Making them today is as difficult as it was then. The batter is so delicious that a large amount of it seems to disappear mysteriously before it even reaches the baking tray.

SECRET INGREDIENTS

MAGIC FORMULA

1 *Pre-heat oven to* 375°F (*Gas Mark* 5) 190°C

2 *Grease a baking tray*

3 *Cream together in large mixing bowl until light and fluffy.* — 75g soft butter
75g brown sugar
75g granulated sugar

4 *With whizz-stick, beat in* — 1 egg
1 tsp vanilla

5 *Sift together and mix in* — 150g plain flour
$\frac{1}{2}$ tsp baking soda
$\frac{1}{2}$ tsp salt

6 *Stir in and mix well* — small packet chocolate dots

7 *Drop batter by teaspoonfuls on to greased baking tray, about* 5cm *apart. Bake* 8–10 *minutes or until golden brown.*

8 *Cool on wire rack and store in airtight tin.*

WHIZZ TRICK

Try adding 50g chopped walnuts with the chocolate dots for cookies with extra crunch.

Honey Mohawks

To this day, no one really knows the identities of the men who took part in the Boston Tea Party. When plans were being made for it, those involved kept all their meetings secret, calling themselves Mohawks and signing all messages with this name. When the Tea Party actually took place, their disguises as Indians made it impossible for anyone to be recognised. The only thing that gave them away afterwards was the odd tea leaf falling out of a shirt cuff or shoe.

These cookies are as secret as the Mohawks because they can be so well disguised that no one will ever guess their true identity. They can carry messages, faces, secret symbols or anything else you feel like sending. The only thing you won't want to disguise is their flavour.

SECRET INGREDIENTS

MAGIC FORMULA

1 *Pre-heat oven to* 350°F (*Gas Mark* 4) 180°C

2 *Grease a baking tray*

3 *Cream together in large mixing bowl until light and fluffy.* — 125g butter, 125g sugar

4 *Beat lightly and blend in* — 1 large egg, pinch salt

5 *Stir in* — 1 rounded tbsp honey, 2 tsp grated orange rind

6 *Sift and stir in, mixing well* — 225g plain flour

7 *Turn dough on to well-floured counter and roll a small amount at a time (with floured rolling pin) to* ½cm *thickness.*

8 *Cut into rounds with a floured biscuit cutter or glass. Lift with a floured palette knife on to a baking tray, then decorate with with warpaint:*

WARPAINT

9 *Mix together in egg cup* — 1 egg yolk, ½ tsp water

10 *Divide mixture between several egg cups or cake cases and make each a different colour with a few drops of* — food colouring

11 *Using a new paintbrush, paint Mohawk faces on the cookies just before they go into the oven.*

12 *Bake just above the centre of the oven for* 12–15 *minutes, or until just lightly coloured.*

Use a palette knife to transfer cookies from the tray to a wire cooling rack. Sprinkle with sugar.

WHIZZ TRICK

If you find the dough too soft to handle, chill it for an hour before rolling.

Hopscotch Brownies

The younger Bostonians, fed up with listening at keyholes and eager to learn what the *The Boston Post Boy** meant by 'trouble brewing up', decided to find out for themselves what was going on. On the pretext of fishing off the wharf, they spent hours watching the ships and their crews. They were determined not to miss anything and when the weather got too cold for fishing, they played endless games of hopscotch on the docks. In between turns they munched brownies and speculated on who would make the next move. It was a long wait but worth it in the end because when the Tea Party did take place, they had ring-side seats.

Though closely related to chocolate brownies, these hopscotch ones are much more fun to make because they turn out differently every time. If you like them soft, add more flour, less, if you like them chewy.

* the local newspaper

SECRET INGREDIENTS

MAGIC FORMULA

1 *Pre-heat oven to* 350°F (*Gas Mark* 4) 180°C

2 *Grease a* 20.5cm *or* 23cm *square baking tin.*

3 *Melt in a saucepan over low heat* ——— 50g butter

4 *Take off the heat and stir in* ——— 175g brown sugar

5 *Leave for a few minutes to cool slightly, then stir in* ——— 1 egg, beaten; ½ tsp vanilla

6 *Sift on to scales then sift together into butter/sugar mixture, blending in well.* ——— 100g plain flour; 1 tsp baking powder; ¼ tsp salt

7 *Stir in* ——— 50g chopped walnuts

8 *Pour batter into greased tin, spreading it out evenly and into the corners with a whizz-stick or spatula.*
Bake 20–25 *minutes or until done* (*use toothpick test*).

9 *Leave to cool then cut into squares. Store in a tightly closed plastic bag or container.*

WHIZZ TRICK

Halve about 12 marshmallows and press them on top of the brownies when you take them out of the oven. Then put under the grill for a few minutes until marshmallows are golden brown. Leave to cool slightly, then slide a knife around the sides to loosen; remove from tin with palette knife, cutting the squares out as you go.

Liberty Punch

When the Mohawks returned from the harbour they were exhausted and very thirsty. To celebrate their success they all got together for a merry toast. In haste, they concocted a punch of whatever came to hand and quite a few hands seemed to be full of tea leaves!

The result was a mixture to please all tastes and just the drink foı any celebration.

SECRET INGREDIENTS

MAGIC FORMULA

1 *Mix together in large jug and stir until sugar is dissolved.*	200ml hot strong tea 75g sugar
2 *When sugar is dissolved, stir in*	200ml orange juice 3 tbsp lemon concentrate (undiluted) 2½ tbsp lime juice
3 *Chill in the refrigerator for at least an hour.*	
4 *Just before serving, add*	1 bottle ginger ale 1 bottle soda water few ice cubes
5 *Pour into glasses and decorate with slices of fresh fruit or sprigs of mint.*	

WHIZZ TRICK

To serve Liberty Punch hot, pour all ingredients except ginger ale, soda water and ice cubes into a medium saucepan. Increase tea to 800ml, sugar to 100g, and add ½ tsp cinnamon and ½ tsp ground cloves. Simmer gently stirring, occasionally, for 5–10 minutes. Pour into cups and serve at once.

DINNER WITH DAVY CROCKETT

MOUNTAIN SOUP

*

POSSUM PIE

*

CORN FRITTERS

*

LEATHER BRITCHES

*

TENNESSEE TATERS

*

RACCOON TAILS

*

PULL TAFFY

*

LOG CABIN

Dinner with Davy Crockett

Having dinner with Davy Crockett isn't quite as easy as it might first appear. For one thing, you can't sit down to dinner afore you find it. None of those big supermarkets round here to get your vittles from. Sometimes takes a whole day to shoot a varmint big enough to fill the stewpot. In the winter, things are different with the critters in hibernation. Then you've got your smokey bacon or salty pork for dinner. There'll be Indian Pudding too or Shoofly Pie – leastways there will be if Davy can swap a few bearskins for sugar and spices.

But just before you get ready to set yourself down, there's a heap of wood to be chopped, cows to be milked and pigs to be fed. After that, you're more'n welcome to be Davy's guest.

Mountain Soup

There's no central heating in your old log cabin and it takes a lot, I reckon, to beat a bowl of hot bean soup for taking the chill off. It's so good you won't even notice these were the same beans you had for last night's supper. First thing you know you'll be wanting second helpings.

SECRET INGREDIENTS

MAGIC FORMULA

1 *Put into deep saucepan and simmer gently for ½ hour.*	1 tin of baked beans 1 tin consommé + 1 tin of water 1 tbsp onion flakes 2 tsp mild mustard 1 tsp brown sugar 1 tsp treacle
2 *Add and simmer for* 30 *minutes more.*	1 tin of tomatoes, mashed
3 *Serve piping hot.*	

WHIZZ TRICK

Butter a slice of stale or toasted bread and cut it to fit the top of the soup bowl. Sprinkle with grated cheese and put under the grill until cheese is brown and bubbling.

Possum Pie

You'll find every sort of wild critter in the Tennessee hills. There's bear, raccoon, and deer, not to mention possum. Now he's a tricky fellow, your possum, 'cos he likes to play dead when he's as alive as could be. He'll just lie there shamming, looking for all the world like an old log. If you're fool enough to pick him up he's just liable to take a bite of your finger! So mind you take care and make sure he's not just 'playin' possum' else you'll have to wait a while for your possum pie. This recipe isn't exactly your real McCoy, as possum is mighty hard to come by these days, but it sure tastes as good.

SECRET INGREDIENTS

MAGIC FORMULA

1 *Put into a large frying pan and cook over medium heat until meat is browned, stirring occasionally to prevent sticking.*	450g minced beef 2 tbsp onion flakes
2 *Lift meat with fish slice on to double square of paper towelling and pour grease in pan into a tin.*	
3 *Put meat back into the frying pan and add, mixing well* *Cook over low heat, stirring from time to time with whizz-stick.*	1 tin of tomato soup +1 tin of water 1 tin of sweet corn 50g grated cheese 1 dessertspoon sugar 1 dessertspoon Worcestershire sauce 1 tsp mild mustard salt and pepper to taste
4 *Fill a saucepan half-full with water, add a teaspoon of salt and bring to the boil. Then add and cook until soft (but not mushy).*	50g cut macaroni
5 *Drain macaroni through a sieve, then stir into meat mixture. Pour into casserole and cover with lid or foil.*	
6 *Bake in the centre of the oven at* 350°F (*Gas Mark* 4) 180°C *for* 30 *minutes or until piping hot.*	
7 *Serve at once, either with Corn Fritters and Leather Britches or on its own.*	

WHIZZ TRICK

To give Possum Pie a crunchy crust, cover it before it goes into the oven with toasted breadcrumbs: crumble 4 slices of stale bread and fry over low heat in 25–50g butter until well-browned.

Corn Fritters

If there's one thing you've got plenty of in these parts it's corn. There'll be corn pone, corn dodgers, hush puppies, mush biscuits, hoecake, hominy grits and heaps of others. A favourite of mine is corn fritters, piping hot from the skillet. You can make them in a minute and they'll vanish just as quick!

SECRET INGREDIENTS

MAGIC FORMULA

1 *Sift together into mixing bowl* —— 8 tbsp self-raising flour
1 tsp salt
¼ tsp pepper

2 *In another bowl, beat until light in colour* —— 1 egg
then mix with —— 100 ml milk

3 *Make a well in the flour mixture and stir in egg mixture gradually with* —— 1 tin of sweet corn (drained)

4 *Heat in heavy frying pan over medium heat until you can smell it.* —— cooking oil (just enough to cover bottom of pan)

5 *Then drop batter in by teaspoonfuls and fry until crisp and golden, turning once with fish slice.*

6 *Drain on paper towelling and serve hot with Possum Pie.*

Leather Britches

If you're looking for the frozen veg, you'll have to get out the ice-pick. No fancy freezers round here. Most times we just dry the veg if we reckon on eating it a few months from now. Take green beans, for instance. Just tie their strings to a pole, leave them in the sun or a dry place and afore you know it, you'll have a whole bucketful of dried beans! Look as tough and leathery as old britches and just about as appetizing until they're cooked. But a few hours in the stewing pot and they're a different kettle of fish!

SECRET INGREDIENTS

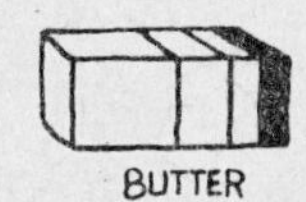

MAGIC FORMULA

1 *Melt in medium saucepan over low heat*	25g butter
2 *Stir in and cook gently until slightly browned.*	1 dessertspoon onion flakes 1 slice ham, torn into small pieces
3 *Fill the saucepan with about* 2cm *of water and bring to the boil. Then add*	225g green beans $1\frac{1}{2}$ tsp sugar $\frac{1}{2}$ tsp salt $\frac{1}{4}$ tsp pepper

4 *Reduce to a low heat, cover with a lid and simmer slowly for* $1\frac{1}{2}$ *hours, stirring occasionally.*

5 *Drain and serve hot or cold.*

Tennessee Taters

I reckon there be just as many taters in Tennessee as there are ears o' corn. Open them up, spoon in a grate of your cheese, a pinch of butter and crispy bacon. Then you're in for a treat, a real Tennessee tater.

SECRET INGREDIENTS

MAGIC FORMULA

1 *Scrub clean* ———————— 4 potatoes

2 *Bake in the oven at* 400°F (*Gas Mark* 6) 200°C *for approximately* 50 *minutes or until they feel soft when you stick a fork into them.*

3 *Take out of the oven and put to one side to cool for a few minutes. Then holding one end of the potato with an oven glove, use your other hand to carefully cut a large cross into the top of the potato.*

4 *Using oven gloves, put one hand at either end of the potato and press towards the centre so that the split opens and the potato pushes out slightly through the middle.*

5 *Carefully spoon into the opening pressing down firmly as you do it.* ——— dollop of butter grated cheese

6 *Then sprinkle over the top* ———— crumbled bacon (well-grilled)

7 *Fill the other* 3 *potatoes in the same way, then pop under the grill for* 2–3 *minutes until the cheese is melted. Serve at once.*

Raccoon Tails

If you've got your eye on Davy's hat, you'll be wanting to go chasing raccoon. Might not be so hard as you think if they get hungry enough. Just leave a bowl of those left-overs outside and they'll come running! But hold on a minute before you start heading for the out of doors. There's a way to track down a dozen or more a whole lot easier. Just rustle up a sugar and butter batter, with a splash of the cooking chocolate. Short while later you'll have more raccoon tails than you can shake a stick at!

SECRET INGREDIENTS

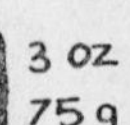

MAGIC FORMULA

1 *Pre-heat oven to* 375°F (*Gas Mark* 5) 190°C

2 *Lightly grease a baking tray*

3 *In a large bowl, cream together until light and fluffy.* —— 75g soft butter
125g sugar

4 *With whizz-stick, beat in* —— 1 egg
grated rind of 1 lemon

5 *Stir in and mix well* —— 150g self-raising flour

6 *Drop dough by teaspoonfuls on to a greased baking tray pressing each one down with the back of spoon into an oblong tail-shape.*

7 *Then grease the back of the spoon, dip in sugar and use it to flatten all the 'tails' (add more sugar as you need it).*

8 *Bake just above the centre of the oven 7–9 minutes or until the edges are a light golden brown. Remove from tray with a palette knife and cool on wire rack.*

CHOCOLATE STRIPES

9 *Melt in top of double saucepan or in a basin over hot water* —— 125g chocolate
50g butter
2 tbsp water

10 *Stir until smooth, then take off the heat and leave to cool until mixture thickens slightly (it should be thick enough for you to drip it on to the cookies without it running off the edges).*

11 *Use a teaspoon to drip chocolate stripes across each tail. (If chocolate gets too thick to 'drip', put it over the heat again, then cool slightly.)*

Pull Taffy

A favourite with all ages, you sure can't beat a good taffy pull! Get the old folks one end, the young 'uns at t'other and p-u-l-l! Bring the ends together and pull agin. Keep this old routine going till the taffy is light in colour. Then everybody gets together to twist the taffy and cut it into bite-sizes. This taffy'll keep you all chewing for some time.

SECRET INGREDIENTS

MAGIC FORMULA

1 *Grease a large plate*

2 *Put into heavy saucepan* —— 225g brown sugar
100g butter
6 level tbsp golden syrup
3 tbsp water
1 tbsp glucose

3 *Stir over low heat until sugar has dissolved.*

4 *Bring to the boil and continue boiling until small amount dropped into a glass of cold water forms a hard ball.*

5 *Pour mixture on to a greased plate and leave to cool slightly.*

6 *When mixture is cool enough to handle, lightly flour your hands and form taffy into a ball. Then pull it out (have a friend take one end if you like), bring back and pull again. Keep this up until taffy is light in colour, then twist and cut with floured scissors into bite-size pieces.*

7 *Wrap in small squares of cling-film and store in a cool place.*

WHIZZ TRICK

For Peppermint Pull Taffy, add 2 teaspoons of peppermint essence in step 5, just before pouring mixture on to plate.

Log Cabin

If you've a mind to build yourself a log cabin, don't just stand there: get a move on! First thing to do is start cutting down as many trees as need be. Strip off all the branches and trim the ends nice and neat. Then cut your notches at each end so they'll fit together. When all the logs are ready, organise yourself a cabin-raisin' with all the neighbours. With the big folks doing the building and the little 'uns filling in the cracks with mud and moss, I'll be jiggered if you don't finish that cabin in a day. Come sundown you'll be sitting in front of the fire as comfy as could be!

SECRET INGREDIENTS

MAGIC FORMULA

1 *In a small bowl, mix together* ——— 75g sifted icing sugar
2 tbsp hot water
1 tbsp cocoa powder

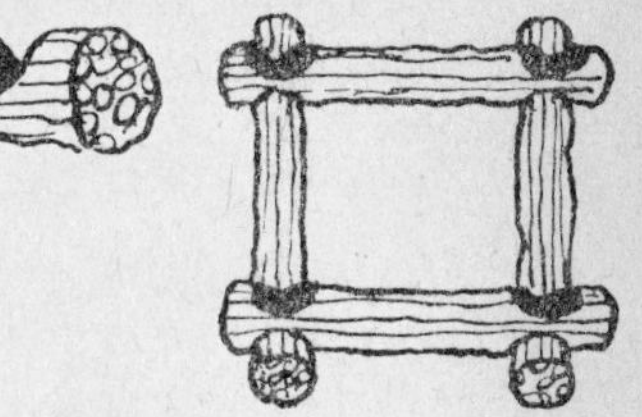

2 *With a blunt knife, carefully saw notches (the width of a chocolate flake) at either end of each chocolate flake.*

3 *Line a baking tray with foil and then build your cabin on it, fitting the logs together. Use the chocolate icing to fill any gaps between the logs.*

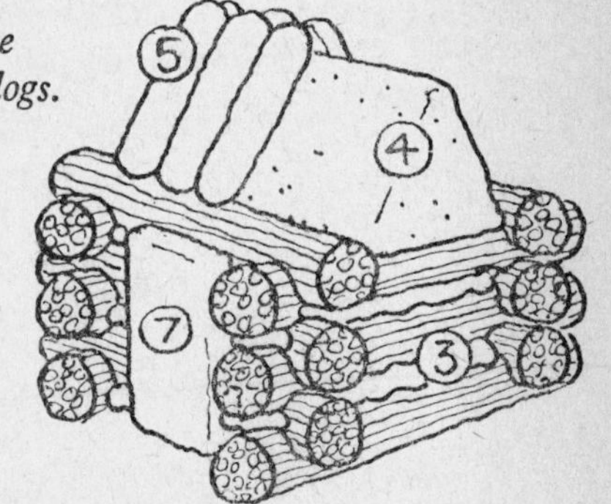

4 *Slice the sides of the cake down from the middle to make it triangular-shaped. Ice the sides lightly with the chocolate mixture. Then carefully place it so that it rests on the logs at either end and is wedged in between the logs which make the side walls.*

5 *Line the chocolate fingers lengthwise side by side on each side of the cake roof. You will have to trim the end of every other one so that they fit together.*

6 *Use the left-over bits of cake to build a chimney against one end of the cabin. Stick them together with the chocolate mixture and then ice it completely when it is finished. Top this with a chocolate biscuit to make a chimney pot and stick the bits trimmed off the chocolate fingers around the base as chimney stones.*

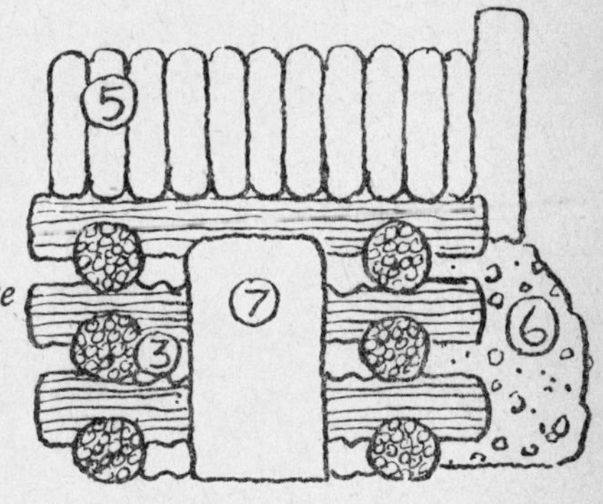

7 *Put a chocolate biscuit in the middle of the front wall as the door. Trim a bit off the bottom if it doesn't stand up straight.*

SMUGGLERS' SNACKS

APPLE FIGGY

*

CORNISH RASCALS

*

GINGER SNAFFLES

*

TREASURE LOAF

*

FOAMING GOLD

*

TOFFEE BARRELS

*

SAILORS' BOOTY

Smugglers' Snacks

If you are suddenly whirled back into the eighteenth century and find yourself somewhere along the Cornish coast, you could be heading for a little excitement. Keep your eyes open if it's a moonless night or if there is a storm brewing, for with customs officers tucked up snugly in their cottages, anything can happen.

When you start exploring, don't be surprised if you come across an old deserted barn or cave which isn't quite as empty as it should be. If it is full of men, huddled together talking and stamping their feet to keep warm, then creep closer to see if you can get a better look.

Apple Figgy

The Master Smuggler is the man you see moving from one group to another. He's responsible for organising this outing. By offering to pay half a guinea, a dollop of tea and all expenses, he has lured over fifty men out in this foul weather. To keep them busy until the signal comes from the cutter off-shore, he has come laden with food and drink. He always brings a few bags of Apple Figgy*, not only because his wife doesn't mind making them but also because they travel so well. Guaranteed to fit all pockets, they can be slipped inside one at a moment's notice, when the men are suddenly needed on the beach or if a customs officer on the prowl interrupts their feast.

* fig is Cornish for raisin

SECRET INGREDIENTS

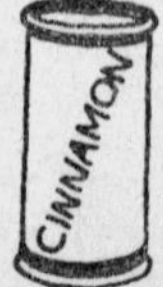

MAGIC FORMULA

1 *Pre-heat oven to* 400°F (*Gas Mark* 6) 200°C

2 *Grease a baking tray*

3 *Using a vegetable peeler, take the skin off* —— 1 cooking apple
Take the core out and cut into chunks.

4 *Fill a small saucepan with* 2cm *of water.*
Add the apple chunks with —— 2½ tbsp brown sugar
and cook over medium heat until the apples are soft, stirring occasionally.
2 tbsp raisins
½ tsp cinnamon
½ tsp mixed spice

5 *Grill until well-browned and drain on paper towelling.* —— 4 sausages

6 *Flour counter lightly and roll out until* ½cm *thick.* —— shortcrust pastry (leave at room temperature for an hour before using)

7 *Put a large saucer down on dough and cut round it to make four circles.*

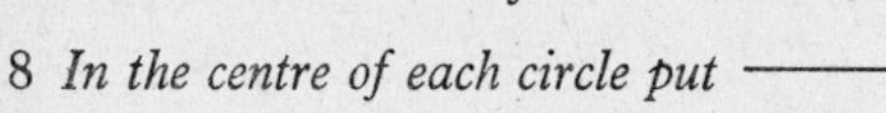

8 *In the centre of each circle put* —— 1 sausage, sliced
1 tbsp apple-raisin mixture

9 *Dampen the edges of the circles with water. Bring the two halves of each circle up to meet each other and pinch together tightly.*

10 *Stand up each Apple Figgy on the baking tray and brush lightly with milk.*

11 *Bake for* 20 *minutes, then reduce heat to* 350°F (*Gas Mark* 4) 180°C *and cook for* 10 *minutes longer.*

Cornish Rascals

The Master Smuggler also brings along an extra supply of Cornish Rascals, just in case the wait is particularly long or the evening especially cold. These are heated up just before he leaves home, wrapped well and then put into saddle bags slung over the horse's back (a good warming oven).

These are typical Rascals in the smuggling world because they look innocent enough but are worth their weight in gold!

SECRET INGREDIENTS

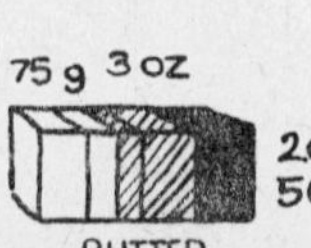

MAGIC FORMULA

1 *Pre-heat oven to* 450°F (*Gas Mark* 8)/230°C

2 *Sift together into mixing bowl* —— 225g self-raising flour, ½ tsp salt

3 *Break into small pieces then rub in until mixture looks like breadcrumbs.* —— 50g butter

4 *Grill until crisp then drain on paper towelling, crumble and mix in.* —— 4 bacon rashers

5 *Mix together until sugar and honey dissolved, then stir in with round-topped knife.* —— 1 tbsp honey, 1 dessertspoon sugar, 125ml milk

6 *Turn dough out on to lightly floured counter and knead lightly for half a minute or until smooth.*

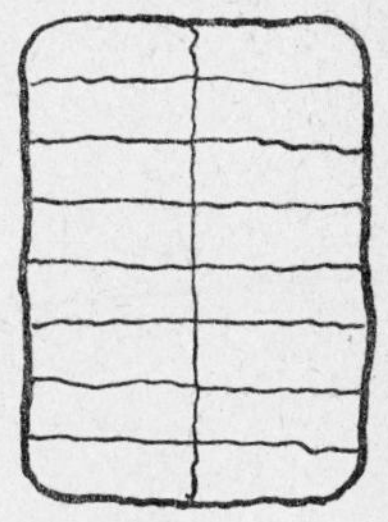

7 *Roll into long oblong shape about* ½cm *thick. Cut in half lengthwise, then cut horizontally into sticks* 2½cm *wide.*

8 *Put into a roasting pan* (30cm × 23cm) *and pop in the oven until melted* —— 75g butter, 2 tbsp honey
Take out and stir until well-blended and evenly distributed in pan.

9 *Place sticks in pan about* ½cm *apart, turning them over once before you put them in the oven so they are well-coated with the honey-butter mixture.*

10 *Bake on top shelf of oven for* 10 *minutes or until golden brown.*

11 *Leave in pan for a minute to soak up butter, then take out with palette knife and put on a plate.*
Serve at once.

Ginger Snaffles

If you can, mingle with the men so you can try one of the Ginger Snaffles. These traditional Cornish biscuits are well-known to smugglers, often under the name of Fairings. It has even been suggested that foreign spices smuggled into Cornwall are responsible for their somewhat exotic flavour.

SECRET INGREDIENTS

MAGIC FORMULA

1 *Pre-heat oven to* 400°F (*Gas Mark* 6) 200°C

2 *Grease a baking tray*

3 *Sift together into large mixing bowl* —— 225g plain flour, sifted
2 tsp ginger
2 tsp mixed spice
2 tsp baking powder
2 tsp baking soda
1 tsp cinnamon
½ tsp salt

4 *Cut into small pieces and rub in.* —— 100g butter

5 *Add and mix well* —— 125g sugar

6 *Heat in small saucepan until warm then stir into dry ingredients.* —— 4 tbsp golden syrup

7 *Flour hands and roll mixture into balls the size of walnuts. Place on greased baking tray about* 5cm *apart.*

8 *Bake on top shelf for* 4 *minutes or until they just start to brown, then move to bottom shelf and cook for another* 4 *minutes.*

9 *Use a palette knife to take them off tray and cool on wire rack. Store in tightly closed container.*

WHIZZ TRICK

To make your Snaffles crunchy, stir in 2 tbsp of chopped candied peel in step 5

Treasure Loaf

A smuggling vessel usually looks remarkably like any other sailing ship. It might not be until a curious customs official comes on board that a dozen barrels of French brandy are discovered under the planks beneath your feet. It might also come as a surprise to find the silks stuffed in hollow oars and the fine linen tumbling out of a false wall in the Captain's cabin!

A Treasure Loaf can play the same tricks on you. At first glance it may look appetizing but perfectly ordinary. However, a practised eye will see straight away that hidden inside are countless smuggled delicacies.

SECRET INGREDIENTS

MAGIC FORMULA

1 *Pre-heat oven to* 300°F (*Mark* 2) 150°C

2 *Grease a* 23cm *loaf tin. Line with greaseproof paper. Grease again.*

3 *Warm together in a saucepan Stir until well-blended, then put to one side to cool slightly.*	4 tbsp golden syrup 2½ tbsp treacle 2 tbsp Ovaltine 150ml milk
4 *Sift together into large mixing bowl*	275g plain flour, sifted 1 tsp baking powder ½ tsp soda ½ tsp salt
5 *Make a well in the flour mixture and stir syrup mixture in, together with*	225g raisins
6 *Beat lightly and stir in gradually*	2 eggs

7 *Pour into greased tin. Bake in the centre of oven for approximately* 1¼ *hours* (*or until done – use the toothpick test*).

8 *Turn out and cool on a wire rack. Slice and serve buttered. Treasure Loaf seems to get better the longer you keep it, if you keep it wrapped in cling-film in a tightly closed tin.*

WHIZZ TRICK

To give Treasure Loaf a good cover, mix together 125g sifted icing sugar and 1 tbsp of lemon or orange juice in a small bowl. Then, using a palette or ordinary knife, ice the top of the loaf with this mixture, letting it drip down the sides like icicles.

Foaming Gold

This gold is the smugglers' speciality and only they know the secret of how to make it double in size at no extra cost! It is equally popular with land and sea smugglers because it can be stored so easily and if carefully wrapped, will last for weeks. If you know the secret, it is a lot easier to get hold of than real gold but unless you keep it secret, you will find it disappears just as quickly.

SECRET INGREDIENTS

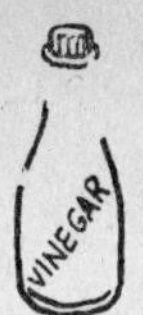

MAGIC FORMULA

1 *Grease* 23cm *square tin with high sides*

2 *Put into a large heavy saucepan and cook over low heat until the butter has melted and the sugar is dissolved, stirring constantly with whizz-stick.* —— 325g sugar
4 level tbsp golden syrup
50g butter
4 tbsp water

3 *Bring to the boil and continue boiling, stirring occasionally to prevent sticking. Test from time to time by dropping a small amount into a glass of cold water. When it forms hard, brittle threads, take off the heat.*

4 *Stir in quickly (this will foam up in the pan)* —— 2 tsp baking soda mixed with 1 tsp vinegar

5 *While still foaming, pour into greased tin, using a spatula to get it all out.*
Then leave tin to cool. Do not move it!

6 *When cool, slide a knife round the edges of the tin to loosen. Then reverse tin on to a plate and gently press the 'gold' out. Break into small pieces by tapping with the back of a spoon.*

7 *Store in a tightly covered tin and keep in a cool place.*

WHIZZ TRICK

For a smaller quantity and a slightly different effect, reduce sugar to 175g, golden syrup to 2 tbsp, butter to 25g, water to 2 tbsp, baking soda to 1 tsp and vinegar to ½ tsp. Pour into small square tin (well-greased).

Toffee Barrels

If you are getting cold feet it's not surprising as you're probably knee-deep in water by now. A rope is usually stretched from the cutter to shore so that the barrels, tied together in pairs, can be swung easily along it. If a customs ship suddenly looms up on the horizon, these 'half-ankers' can be quickly tied to the rope and lowered below the water surface. They are then retrieved some time later, when the customs men are not around to claim more than their fair share.

These toffee barrels make excellent loot. If you have a surplus on your hands, swap them with fellow smugglers for Foaming Gold or Cornish Rascals.

SECRET INGREDIENTS

MAGIC FORMULA

1 *Grease a* 19cm *square tin*

2 *Melt in large heavy saucepan over very low heat* ——— 75g butter

3 *Stir in* ——— 300ml condensed milk
175g sugar
1 tbsp golden syrup

4 *Stirring constantly, cook over <u>a very low heat</u> until the mixture thickens and becomes a rich brown toffee colour.*

5 *Take off the heat and add* ——— 1 tsp vanilla

6 *Mix well, then pour into greased tin. Mark into squares.*

7 *When cool, slide a round-topped knife along the edges of the tin to loosen, then lift the squares out with a palette knife. Roll each one between your fingers lightly to curve the sides into a barrel shape.*

Wrap each toffee barrel in a piece of greaseproof paper or cling-film. Store in a tightly closed plastic container or tin.

WHIZZ TRICK

For a more unusual toffee barrel, add a squirt of lemon juice in step 5.

Sailors' Booty

Once all the barrels and bales are on shore, there is still a long night's work ahead. If you are a tubcarrier, you will have to carry one barrel on your back and another on your front to balance it. Their destination could be the next cove or a churchyard five miles away! When you have delivered them to their final hiding-place, it is time to collect your payment and head for home. Just the moment, perhaps, to reach in your pocket and get out the Sailors' Booty.

This midnight snack was first concocted by sea smugglers who dreamt up every possible way to eat fish on their voyages. In real smuggler style, the booty is stuffed with gold, but this time it's in cheese form.

SECRET INGREDIENTS

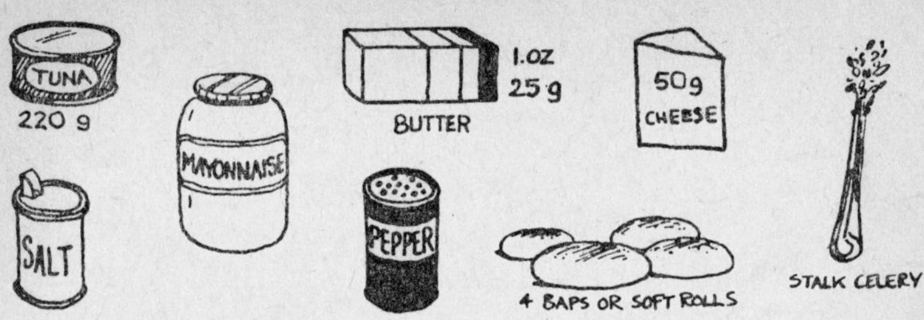

MAGIC FORMULA

1 *Pre-heat oven to* 375°F (*Gas Mark* 5) 190°C

2 *Mix together in large bowl* —— 1 tin tuna, well-drained of oil
50g grated cheese
3 tbsp mayonnaise
3 tbsp finely diced celery
salt and pepper to taste

3 *Cut in half* —— 4 large soft rolls
butter and fill with tuna mixture.

4 *Wrap each filled roll in a square of foil. Put on a baking tray and into the oven.*

5 *Bake* 20 *minutes or until piping hot.*
Serve at once.

WHIZZ TRICK

For a slightly pink Sailors' Booty, use tinned salmon (drained) instead of tuna and the taste is just as good!

ESKIMORSELS

IGLOODLE

*

POLAR BEAR SANDWICH

*

HOKEY-POKEY

*

ESKIMO PIES

*

LEMON WHIZZ CREAM

*

ESKI-ROLL

*

MILK SNOZZLE

Eskimorsels

There are bound to be times in your career of Kitchen Wizardry when you get so steamed up that you never want to see another hot dish, hot pot or hot stove again. When this happens, don't dive into the deep freeze, head for the North Pole instead.

The Pole is the home of The Whizz Cream Machine, an extraordinary ice-cream making operation. This machine churns out more kinds of ice-cream than you've ever made magic potions. Built up like a mountain around it are layers of snow and ice so that mixtures made in its bottom half are frozen solid and those in the top half come out as soft whip. It is controlled by an Elder Eski-Chef who decides whether to try out a new recipe or put through one of the old favourites. Junior Tasters are on the spot to give a first-hand opinion the minute a fresh batch comes through.

Spies are sent in regularly from ice-cream companies all over the world but so far have only come out with cold noses and empty hands. But thanks to a friendly Eski-chef, a number of top Eskimorsel recipes have been smuggled out of the country and are published for the first time on the following pages. It is impossible to say which are the Eski-Favourites as they seem to like them all!

Igloodle

Scattered round The Whizz Cream Machine are igloo-kitchens devoted to the trial and tasting of new ice-cream recipes. Just to give you an idea of what goes on inside, let's slip into the Ice-cream in Shapes kitchen for a minute. Here they are working on a project which involves designing a completely edible igloo. The latest idea is to make the outer formation from crispy cereal and marshmallow with a centre of vanilla ice-cream. Why don't you join in and experiment with this version? Then you can dream up ways of building your own custom-built igloo.

SECRET INGREDIENTS

MAGIC FORMULA

1 *Grease a large square or oblong baking tin.*

2 *Melt in a large saucepan over low heat stirring all the time to prevent sticking.* —— 30 white marshmallows, 50g butter/margarine

3 *When completely melted, take off the heat and add* —— 1 tsp vanilla

4 *Then stir in quickly and mix until completely covered with marshmallow mixture.* —— 150g Rice Crispies

5 *Pour straight into greased tin and press mixture down evenly with your fingers.*

6 *Mark into squares and as soon as the mixture is cool enough to handle, take them out one by one to construct the igloo.*

7 *First form a small circle on a baking tray, standing the squares up with two pointing outwards to make the doorway.*

Then build another layer on top, pressing the squares together to seal. When you get to the third layer, slant the squares over slightly and press together to form the curved roof.

Put two squares down flat over the doorway to cover it.

You must work as quickly as you can for the longer you leave the squares, the harder they will be to mould into shape. If they do get too hard to shape, then just pop them back into the oven for a few minutes to soften.

8 *Put the finished igloo on a square of foil. To give it a bit of colour, make a small flag, attach it to a toothpick and plant it gently in the igloo roof.*

When ready to eat Igloodle, fill the centre with ice-cream and slice as you would a pie.

Polar Bear Sandwich

The only problem with the outdoor storage system is that it tends to encourage frequent polar bear picnics. The polar bear nose is capable of tracking down ice-cream in any flavour, in any shape and at any distance. The bears usually don't even wait until the ice-cream is frozen. They just sample it straight away! Their claws are tailor-made for prying the tops off storage caves and within minutes they have gobbled up three or four gallons of the choicest ice-cream.

One recipe in particular seems to be their favourite and in view of the great quantities they consume it is now known as Polar Bear Sandwich.

SECRET INGREDIENTS

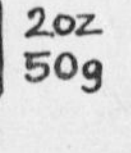

MAGIC FORMULA

1 *Line an* 20.5cm *or* 23cm *loaf tin with foil.*

2 *Melt together in double saucepan or in basin over hot water stirring from time to time.*	24 white marsh-mallows 125ml milk
3 *Stir in then put into the refrigerator to cool slightly.*	2 tsp peppermint essence a few drops green food colouring
4 *Put into plastic bag, tie tightly and crush to crumbs with rolling pin.*	16 filled chocolate biscuits
5 *Melt over low heat in saucepan then take off the heat, stir in biscuit crumbs and put to one side.*	50g butter
6 *Whip until soft peaks form then fold into cooled marshmallow mixture with metal spoon.*	275ml double cream

7 *Cover bottom of loaf tin with a light sprinkling of biscuit crumbs. Then cover with a layer of marshmallow mixture, a layer of crumbs, another layer of marshmallow and finish up with a layer of crumbs. If you have any marshmallow mixture left over, finish up with a layer of that instead.*

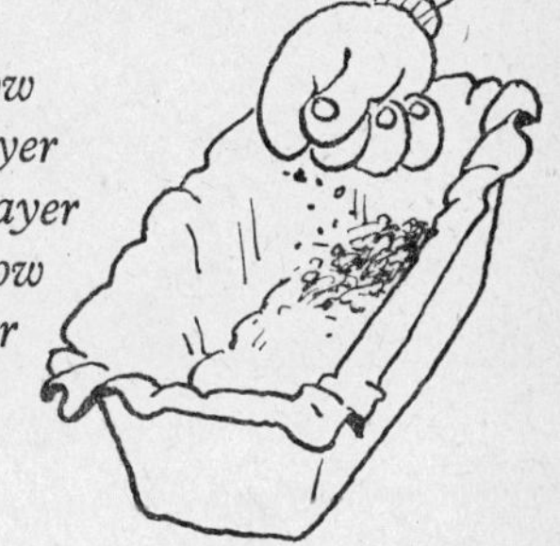

8 *Cover with foil and put into the freezing compartment of the refrigerator.*

9 *Freeze* 4–5 *hours or overnight.*

10 *To serve, reverse tin on to a plate. Take off the foil and slice as you would a loaf of bread.*

Hokey-Pokey

Occasionally the Machine has an off day when it produces ice-cream the texture of soup. This soupy mixture is poured into a special vat and the Fix-it Chef is sent for. His usual remedy is to add whipped cream and lots of custard to help it freeze. This is then mixed well and poured into one of the large snow freezers.

Any ice-cream like this which is easy and cheap to make has always been called Hokey-Pokey, even in the North Pole.

SECRET INGREDIENTS

LARGE TIN

OR WHIPPING CREAM

1.oz
25 g
BUTTER

MAGIC FORMULA

Turn freezing compartment to its coldest setting a few hours before you need to use it.

1 *Melt in a saucepan over low heat stirring constantly with whizz-stick.*	150g brown sugar 25g butter ¼ tsp salt
2 *Add and mix in well then let it come to the boil and boil gently for* 5–10 *minutes or until thick and syrupy, stirring occasionally.*	125ml hot water
3 *Take off the heat and leave to cool slightly.*	
4 *Gradually stir in and mix until well-blended.*	275g thick custard
5 *Whip until standing in soft peaks*	275ml double cream

6 *Using spatula or metal spoon, fold sugar/custard mixture into the cream.*

7 *Pour into plastic container with a lid and put straight into the freezing compartment.*

8 *Freeze* 2–3 *hours or until firm. Then turn freezer back to normal temperature.*

WHIZZ TRICK

To make a Hokey-Pokey Cake, line the bottom of plastic container with sponge fingers, then pour in half the ice-cream mixture (unfrozen). Top this with another layer of sponge fingers and then the remaining Hokey-Pokey. Freeze until solid, then slide a knife round the edges to loosen and cut into slices Just take out as much as you can eat at one time and put the rest back immediately into the freezer.

Eskimo Pies

As with any cooking operation, there are always a certain number of disasters at the Pole but here is proof that they sometimes work out for the best.

One day a young Eski-chef, eager to cool off a large quantity of chocolate sauce quickly, poured it straight into an empty freezer. He soon discovered it wasn't quite as empty as he thought when another Eski-chef arrived to find his precious Super Vanilla Ice-cream now drowned in chocolate sauce! While he threw himself into the nearest snowbank, the first chef hurriedly had all the ice-cream dug out and carted away at his own expense. He then invited all his neighbours round to help finish it off. To his surprise, it was a huge success and the queue for seconds stretched the length of three igloos. By popular demand the recipe went into official production and in no time at all became one of the top Eski-sellers. Without knowing it, he had created the first Eskimo Pie.

SECRET INGREDIENTS

MAGIC FORMULA

Turn freezing compartment to its coldest setting a few hours before you need to use it.

1 *Cut out 9 circles of foil and line patty tin sections with them.*

2 *Very quickly fill 9 cake cases $\frac{2}{3}$ full with*—vanilla ice-cream
Level off the tops with the back of a spoon and put straight into the freezer.

3 *When they are frozen solid, start the chocolate coating. Melt together* ——— 150g cooking chocolate
50g butter
$2\frac{1}{2}$ tbsp water
in top of double saucepan or in basin over hot water.
When completely melted, blend well together and take off the heat.
Leave to cool slightly.

4 *Pour slightly cooled chocolate into each lined section, until about just over half full.*

5 *Take the filled cake cases out of the freezer, one at a time, and remove the paper. Press ice-cream firmly into each section so that the chocolate is pushed up round the sides.*
Carefully pour a little more chocolate on top, just enough to cover the ice-cream completely.
Do this for all the pies.

6 *Try to cover all the pies as quickly as you can so that the ice-cream doesn't melt. Then pop the patty tins into the freezer and leave until frozen solid.*

7 *If the patty tins take up too much room in your freezer, take the pies out when frozen, wrap each one in a square of foil and put straight back into the freezer.*

Lemon Whizz Cream

With so much ice-cream within easy reach, residents of the Pole can hardly complain. But they do occasionally get tired of all the fancy Eskimorsels and long for something simple. So, one day every month, the Machine is switched on to 'ice-cream ordinaire' and in no time produces the most delicious concoction of Lemon Whizz Cream. Guaranteed to settle any stomach, it is the best Polar Medicine yet invented.

SECRET INGREDIENTS

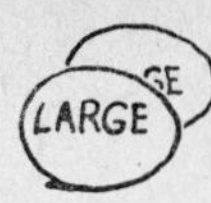

MAGIC FORMULA

1 *Cut in half and squeeze the juice of* —— 2 lemons

2 *Pour into a small bowl and beat together with* —— 2 egg yolks, pinch salt

3 *In another bowl, beat until standing in soft peaks* —— 275 ml double cream

4 *With metal spoon, fold in* —— 50g sugar

5 *In third bowl, beat until stiff* —— 2 egg whites

6 *Fold in* —— 125g sugar

7 *Fold lemon/yolk mixture into whipped cream and then fold in the beaten egg whites.*

8 *When completely blended, pour into a plastic container with a lid and put straight into the freezer.*
Freeze until firm.

WHIZZ TRICK

For special occasions, pour Whizz Cream into a round container lined with foil. Freeze until firm, then just before serving, reverse on to a plate. Remove the foil and decorate with whipped cream, coloured sparkles or chocolate shavings.

Eski-Roll

One of the most exciting moments at the Pole has been the discovery of the Eski-Roll. This makes it possible for Eski-chefs to take ice-cream making seriously and play a few practical jokes at the same time. A favourite trick of the younger chefs is to hide the ice-cream in Eskimorsels so well that it turns up when you least expect it. They especially like to try this out on unsuspecting visitors, so be on your guard. Eski-Roll is ideally suited for this trick as it looks suspiciously like a large slice of snowbank. It is only when you take a brave bite into it that you strike vanilla ice-cream rolled up in a chocolate sponge!

SECRET INGREDIENTS

MAGIC FORMULA

1 *Pre-heat oven to* 375°F (*Gas Mark* 5) 190°C

2 *Grease a small swiss roll tin* (*approx.* 34cm×24cm.) *and line with greaseproof paper. Grease again.*

3 *Fill a medium saucepan* ⅓ *full of water and bring to the boil. Take off the heat and place on a tea-towel laid flat on a table to keep the saucepan from slipping.*

4 *Put in a basin which will fit snugly into the top of the saucepan* ——— 3 eggs
Beat with rotary or electric beater 75g sugar
until thick and creamy (*and will leave a clear trail when beater is lifted out*).

5 *Sift on to scales* ——— 50g self-raising flour
then sift together into egg/sugar mixture. 3 level tbsp cocoa
Carefully fold in with metal spoon

6 *Pour mixture into greased tin and spread evenly with a spatula. Bake in the centre of the oven* 12–15 *minutes or until it feels springy to the touch.*

7 *Turn the cake out on to a piece of greaseproof paper sprinkled with caster sugar, on top of a tea-towel. Peel off the greaseproof paper lining. Roll up tightly in greaseproof paper and tea-towel and leave to cool.*

8 *When cool, carefully unroll and spread quickly with* ——— vanilla ice-cream
Roll up tightly and wrap in a square of foil. Put straight into freezing compartment.

9 *Freeze* 3–4 *hours. To serve, remove foil and slice as you would a swiss roll.*

WHIZZ TRICK

For a special Peppermint Eski-Roll, grate a bar of mint chocolate and sprinkle over the ice-cream. Roll up and ice with a mixture of 1 dessertspoon caster sugar and 1 tsp peppermint essence folded into 150ml double cream, whipped stiff.

Milk Snozzle

Surrounded by ice-cream the Eski-kids turn up their noses at drinking plain milk. They pride themselves on their endless Milk Snozzle concoctions and have listed a few here for you to try:

Whisk up together:

Milk	+blackcurrant syrup	+vanilla ice-cream	
Milk	+blackcurrant syrup	+strawberry ice-cream	
Milk	+orange juice	+vanilla ice-cream	
Milk	+peach juice (or mashed peaches)	+vanilla ice-cream	
Milk	+drinking chocolate or chocolate syrup	+chocolate ice-cream	
Milk	+drinking chocolate or chocolate syrup	+vanilla ice-cream	+peppermint essence
Milk	+mashed banana	+vanilla ice-cream	
Milk	+raspberries	+vanilla ice-cream	
Milk	+strawberries	+strawberry ice-cream	
Milk	+lemon squash	+vanilla ice-cream	

The Eski-kids always adjust the flavourings to suit their taste. But the proportions are usually 175ml milk to 2 tbsp flavouring, fruit or syrup, to 1 large scoop of ice-cream.

Try experimenting with various combinations and quantities and you will be a Snozzle-expert in no time.

SECRET INGREDIENTS

MAGIC FORMULA

1 *Put into a large clean jar and screw the top on tightly.* —— 175ml cold milk
2 tbsp raspberries (with their juice)
1 large scoop vanilla ice-cream
½ dessertspoon sugar

2 *Using both hands, shake the jar back and forth vigorously for* 1 *minute.*

3 *Pour straight into a tall glass, sip it through a straw or drink as is!*

To make the Milk Snozzles listed on the opposite page, use this as your basic recipe and substitute the various different flavourings and ice-creams.

Mr Popper's Penguins

FLORENCE AND RICHARD ATWATER

All through the summer Mr Popper paints people's houses, but when winter comes, he stays at home reading books on polar exploration. Mr Popper longs to be an explorer, and this leads him to write a letter to his hero Admiral Drake at the South Pole. In return Admiral Drake sends him a present – marked 'Keep Cool' – which contains a lively penguin named Captain Cook who moves into the fridge. But this is only the beginning before long, there are eleven more penguins in the Popper household!

'These events are treated as normal and quite understandable happenings, and the humour arises from this matter of fact acceptance, which appeals greatly to children.'
Sheila Ray, Children's Fiction

'It bounces gaily from hilarity to hilarity.' *School Librarian*

Delightful reading for sevens and up.

The Boy Who Sprouted Antlers

JOHN YEOMAN AND QUENTIN BLAKE

'As long as you set your mind on it and try hard enough, there's nothing you can't do,' said Miss Beddows to Billy when he declared that he simply couldn't make a basket. Billy liked the idea that he could do anything, but Melanie and Paul didn't agree.

'What about growing horns?' said Melanie. It was a challenge that Billy had to accept.

'Wildly improbable and cleverly sustained.' *Margery Fisher*

Hilarious reading for sevens and up.

Dominic

WILLIAM STEIG

'What a wonderful world,' thought Dominic as he set out, all senses alert, on the highroad to adventure. And when he met the witch-alligator he quickly took her advice. 'Up this road,' she said, 'things will happen that you could never have guessed at – marvellous, unbelievable things. Up this way is where adventure is.' Now up that road and round the corner lurked the notorious Doomsday Gang, ready and scheming to trick passersby. But in Dominic, a talented dog inspired by action, they finally met their match.

William Steig, winner of the Caldecott Award, has written and illustrated this fantasy for children of nine and up.